The Popular Guide
to the Bible

The Popular Guide to the Bible

A GUIDE TO THE GREATEST BOOK EVER WRITTEN

Bret Winter

Various scriptures used in this text are from the Holy Bible, New International Version ®, NIV® Copyright © 1973, 1978, 1984 by Biblica, Inc.® Used by permission. All rights reserved worldwide. All pictures in this book are in the public domain and are not under copyright restrictions.
ISBN: 1519236336
ISBN 13: 9781519236333

Dedicated to the *'Word who became Flesh and dwelt among us,*
Full of grace and truth.'
John 1:14

.

Introduction

§

THE BIBLE, THE *"WORD OF GOD"* is the most influential book in the history of mankind, it is also the most read book in the entire world! The Bible was written over a period of 1500 years from around 1400B.C. to 90 A.D. by more than 40 different writers, living in the present day regions of the Middle East, Africa and Europe. In this book, we learn about all facets of human existence, everything from the creation of the universe and mankind, to theology, philosophy, history, poetry, prophecy, war, romance, love, adventure and miracles. Even today it sells tens of millions of copies every year in almost every language on earth. When initially looking at the basics of this book we should know the word *'Bible'* is an English word from the Latin language meaning *Biblical* or *the Books*. The first Christians began to us the term *Bible* or the term *the Books* sometime in the 2nd century, but it really wasn't until the 3rd and early 4th centuries that the book we have today was fully accepted by the Church as *"Canon Text."* The word *Canon* comes from the Greek language which means *measuring stick* or *ruler.* Consequently, the Bible we have today is known as the *ruler* or foundational measuring stick of the Judeo-Christian Faith. In 2nd Timothy 3:16 we are told *"All scripture is God breathed and is useful for all teaching, rebuking, correcting and training in righteousness,"* so the importance of knowing this book is immeasurable for everyone! The standard Bible we have today is made up of 66 books, 39 from the Old Testament (the Jewish Bible) and 27 from the New Testament (which is the divinely inspired and authoritative writings about Jesus Christ), accordingly, the word *Testament* can also mean *Covenant*, which means a legal agreement between two parties. In the case of the Bible (the Old and New Testaments) it is a *'unilateral covenant'* from God to man. The reader should always understand this *'unilateral covenant'* from God to man is the main theme throughout all of Scripture. In this guide we will look at the 66 books in the traditional order and provide you, the reader, a basic scenario of the content of each book and its relevance to everyone today, also as we study each book several Scriptures will be noted and a commentary given underneath each of them. This commentary is for everyone, it is for Christians, Jews, Muslims, Atheists, Agnostics or any individual who has any interest in knowing the essentials of the Bible, but the reader should always remember when studying the Bible the central theme is continually God's desire to have fellowship with you!

Table of Contents

Introduction · vii

The Old Testament · 1
Genesis · 3
Exodus · 9
Leviticus · 14
Numbers · 17
Deuteronomy · 19
Joshua · 23
Judges · 25
Ruth · 27
1st Samuel · 30
2nd Samuel · 33
1st Kings · 36
2nd Kings · 39
1st Chronicles · 42
2nd Chronicles · 44
Ezra · 46
Nehemiah · 48
Esther · 51
Job · 54
The Psalms · 57
The Proverbs · 59
Ecclesiastes · 62
Song of Songs · 66
Isaiah · 68

Jeremiah · 71

Lamentations · 74

Ezekiel · 76

Daniel · 78

Hosea · 82

Joel · 84

Amos · 86

Obadiah · 88

Jonah · 90

Micah · 93

Nahum · 95

Habakkuk · 97

Zephaniah · 99

Haggai · 101

Zechariah · 103

Malachi · 105

The New Testament · 107

The Gospel of Matthew · 109

The Gospel of Mark · 114

The Gospel of Luke · 117

The Gospel of John · 123

Acts · 130

Romans · 137

1st Corinthians · 141

2nd Corinthians · 144

Galatians · 147

Ephesians · 150

Philippians · 153

Colossians · 155

1st Thessalonians · 157

2nd Thessalonians · 160

Titus · 162

Philemon · 164

Hebrews · 166

James · 169

1st Peter · 171
2nd Peter · 175
1st John · 178
2nd John · 181
3rd John · 183
Jude · 185
Revelation · 187

The Old Testament

Genesis

§

Author and Date   The author of the book of Genesis was Moses, the word '*Genesis*' means '*Origins*' or '*Beginning*.' The book was most likely written around 1400 B.C., after the time Moses led the Israelites out of Egypt.

Synopsis   The Book of Genesis can rightly be divided into two sections, the "Primeval History" section and the "Patriarchal History" section. In the *Primeval history* section of Genesis we learn about the creation story, the fall of man, Noah and the flood, and the dispersion of mankind around the world. In the *Patriarchal history* section, we learn about the lives of the Patriarchs; Abraham, Isaac, Jacob and his 12 sons. In the *Primeval history* section, God creates the heavens, the earth and humanity. In the creation of mankind we learn the primary reason why God creates man is to have fellowship with him. Unfortunately, in the course of time Adam and Eve (the first man and woman) disobey God and sin, therefore bring-ing separation from God, and death into the world. After this disobedience, we see mankind multiplying upon the earth and evil increasing in the world until there was only one family living in the entire world in which God finds any good. Because of this, God reluctantly sends a flood to destroy humanity, but saves the righteous Noah and his family, along with the earth's animals. He does this by having Noah build an Ark, which floats upon the waters until the flood dissipates. After the flood ceases they live in a new world and begin to prosper and multiply. Long after the flood, and mankind increasing throughout the world, we enter into the Patriarchal age, where God chooses a man named Abraham, who was a descendant of Noah. In Abraham, the Lord God creates a chosen people to bring God's blessing to all of mankind. The reason for this chosen line of people coming into the world through

Abraham was so God could bring his '*Word, laws and promises to the world*,' which in turn brings the promised Messiah (Christ) to mankind. Initially, the chosen line would pass from Abraham to his son Isaac, and then to Isaac's son Jacob, and then to Jacob's offspring. Through Jacob's offspring, his twelve sons would become the nation of Israel! Toward the end of Genesis we read a great story of God's sovereignty and preservation of the chosen people. One of Jacobs's sons named Joseph is taken to Egypt through the despicable actions of his brothers. In this horrible act, Joseph was sold as a slave and taken to Egypt, but fortunately by God's miraculous design, Joseph the slave, eventually rises to rule over all of Egypt and eventually saves Jacob, his brothers and their families from a devastating famine which came upon the region. In this story we learn it is through Joseph's God-given gifts that ensure the survival of the promised lineage of God's people. As Genesis concludes, and the book of Exodus begins, we should always remember that Genesis is primarily about the covenant promises from God to his people. The promises of God lay the enduring foundation of the rest of the Bible!

Notable Verses

Genesis 1:1

"*In the beginning God created the heavens and the earth*."
These are the opening words of the Bible and the declaration that God created everything! There is a lot of discussion and ideas about when this actually occurred and how it happened, but what we do know is the Lord God Almighty was the author of it all!

Genesis 1:27

"*So God created man in his own image, in the image of God he created him; male and female he created them*."
In this verse of Scripture we learn that man was created in God's image and likeness! We see that the '*Creator*' of the universe is a person as we are, and '*man*' is the crowning achievement of His creation.

**In this famous picture we see a metaphor of God
creating man in his image and likeness.**

Genesis 1:31
"And God saw everything that he had made, and, behold, it was very good. And the evening and the morning were the sixth day."
Here, we understand that the Lord God looked over His creation and was glad! His creative power is at work in the world even today.

Genesis 2:18
"The Lord God said, it is not good for the man to be alone; I will make for him a help-mate."
In this verse, God sees the loneliness of man and creates a woman to be his companion and friend, in doing this God creates marriage and the first family.

Genesis 6:6-7
"And it grieved the LORD that he had made man on the earth, and it troubled him in his heart. And the LORD said, I will destroy man whom I have created from the face of the earth; both man, and beast, and the creeping thing, and the fowls of the air; for I regret that I have made them."
At one point in the history of mankind, God was displeased with His creation and sent a worldwide flood, however, He found a righteous man in Noah.

Noah and his sons build the Ark

Genesis 12:2-3
" And I will make of you a great nation, and I will bless you, and make your name great; and you shall be a blessing: And I will bless them that bless you, and curse him that curses you: and in you shall all families of the earth be blessed."
In this verse, we see a great promise God gives to Abraham the Patriarch. Abraham and his blessing remain upon God's people, even today!

Genesis 22:2
"And he said, Take now your son, your only son Isaac, whom you love, and go to the land of Moriah; and offer him there for a burnt offering upon one of the mountains which I will tell you of."

In this verse we see the great faith of Abraham in obeying God. God is pleased when we show faith in our lives.

Abraham and Isaac in the sacrifice story

Genesis 35:22
"Jacob had Rueben, Simeon, Levi, Judah, Issachar, Zebulun, Joseph, Benjamin, Dan, Naphtali, Gad and Asher"
Here we learn about the 12 tribes of Israel being brought forth by the Patriarch Jacob, interestingly, Jesus Christ came from the tribe of Judah which fulfilled many biblical prophecies.

Genesis 50:20
" But as for you, all of you thought evil against me; but God meant it for good, to bring to pass, as it is this day, to save many people"

In the inspirational life of Joseph, we learn a great lesson on how to be merciful toward all. The story of Joseph is one of the most powerful in all the Bible about remaining faithful to God regardless of what circumstance we find our self in.

Exodus

§

Author and Date   Moses was the author of the book of Exodus, the book of Exodus was likely written around 1400 B.C. The word Exodus means *'Departure'* and in this case it specifically means the departure of the children of Israel from Egypt!

Synopsis   Exodus begins where the book of Genesis leaves off, with God dealing with His chosen people, the Israelites. It traces the events from the time of Jacob and his children when they entered Egypt until they were eventually delivered from their bondage after 400 years of slavery. In the first section of the book of Exodus we learn of the treatment of the Israelites in Egypt under Pharaoh. We also read about the early life of Moses and his rise as Israel's leader. The primary *'call'* of Moses on his life by God is that he is to be the one who leads Israel from their slavery under the Egyptians. The process of Moses becoming the leader of Israel is absolutely miraculous, for God himself brings about many devastating plagues to the unrepentant Egypt. After these terrifying plagues occur upon a reluctant Egypt, we see the actual *'Exodus'* of the children of Israel from the land. Throughout this section of the book, God's powerful hand is seen in many supernatural occurrences, ending with the plague of the death to the *'firstborn'* in all of Egypt. Interestingly, in this plague against the *'firstborn'* of Egypt, the only firstborn children who survived were those families who rubbed lambs blood on the doorposts of their homes. The act of rubbing innocent blood on the doorways caused the angel of death *"passing over"* the Israelite houses, which gave them reprieve from God's judgment. This historic act gave God's people a significant religious holiday known as *"Passover,"* which is a special Jewish holiday even practiced today! After the historic event of *"Passover"* in Exodus, we also see things like the actual departure of the Israelites from Egypt, the parting of the Red Sea, and the destruction of the Egyptian army. In the central section of the book of *'Exodus'* we learn of the actual wanderings of the people of Israel in the desert and the miraculous provision God provides them. At this time

God gives the Israelites supernatural food called manna from heaven. He also gives them miraculous water in the desert, victory over their enemies, and the famous *'Ten Commandments.'* Also fascinating at this time is when the Lord gives supernatural daily navigation to the Israelites in the form of a *'pillar of fire by night'* and a *'pillar of cloud by day.'* As we learn of God's blessings to the people in this part of Exodus we also unfortunately read that even with all these miracles many Israelites of this generation sinned and rebelled against the Lord. The last section of the book gives us insight into the making of the *'Ark of the Covenant'* and the plan for the *'Tabernacle,'* with all the pertinent ceremonies, rituals and corresponding furnishings that will be needed for the worship of God.

Notable Verses

Exodus 3:6
"Moreover he said, I am the God of your father, the God of Abraham, the God of Isaac, and the God of Jacob. And Moses hid his face; for he was afraid to look upon God"
Here we have a powerful statement by God Himself concerning the covenant He made with the children of Israel through Abraham, Isaac and Jacob. Later we learn God's covenant with Abraham was thoroughly fulfilled in Christ, with God's blessings being promised to those who receive him by faith!

Exodus 6:6
"Wherefore say unto the children of Israel, I am the LORD, and I will bring you out from under the burdens of the Egyptians, and I will rid you out of their bondage, and I will redeem you with a stretched out arm, and with great judgments."
Here we see the Lord God telling the people of Israel that their captivity was over, and that God himself would deliver them. The *'Exodus'* from Egypt would soon take place after this statement by the Lord.

Exodus 12:27
"That all of you shall say, it is the sacrifice of the LORD's Passover, who passed over the houses of the children of Israel in Egypt, when he struck the Egyptians, and delivered our houses. And the people bowed the head and worshipped."

Here we learn about the beginning of the famed '*Passover*' holiday being instituted among the children of Israel, this magnificent observance is practiced by many today.

Exodus 15:26
"For I am the Lord, who heals you."
In this verse, we are given an outstanding promise by God!   He is always ready and willing to heal and bless His people.

Exodus 20:2-3
" I am the LORD your God, which have brought you out of the land of Egypt, out of the house of bondage. You shall have no other gods before me."
In this verse, we understand the first commandment of God, and the most important, which is to keep the Lord God pre-eminent in our lives.

In this symbolic picture Moses receives the Ten Commandments from God

Exodus24:8

"And Moses took the blood, and sprinkled it on the people, and said; Behold the blood of the covenant, which the LORD has made with you concerning all these words."
In this verse, we see how the people of God used the blood of animals as a religious ceremony to purify from sins. Since Christ came to mankind, we cleanse ourselves from sin by embracing the atoning work of Christ and the Cross! He is our sacrificial lamb, which takes away our sins and give us right standing with God.

Exodus34:6-7

And the LORD passed by before him, and proclaimed, "The LORD, The LORD God, merciful and gracious, longsuffering, and abundant in goodness and truth, Keeping mercy for thousands, forgiving iniquity and transgression and sin. And that will by no means clear the guilty; visiting the iniquity of the fathers upon the children, and upon the children's children, unto the third and to the fourth generation. "
In this great verse of scripture, we learn some fantastic attributes of God Almighty, first of all He is compassionate and gracious, and filled with love for all! He shows us this by being slow to condemn us for our sins and imperfections and always helping us to live good lives. He wants us to turn from sin because He loves us and knows that sin has the power to bring significant harm and destruction to us in our lives.

The children of Israel leaving Egypt after 400 years of bondage.

Leviticus

§

Author and Date The famed Moses was the author of the book of Leviticus, it was written around 1400 B.C., interestingly, the word Leviticus means; *'relating to the Levites,'* which was the priestly tribe of Israel.

Synopsis The Israelites had been held in captivity in Egypt for around 400 years, because of this many of the descendants of Abraham, Isaac and Jacob did not know about the Lord God and his ways. Leviticus instructs the Israelites on how to be righteous and holy in the sight of God, the God that many of them did not even know! The emphasis in Leviticus is how to be personally *'Holy'* before God through ritual and ceremony. The reason behind many of these rituals was that man as a sinful and imperfect person must have a covering to deal with a *'Holy God.'* So through the offering of acceptable sacrifices, special diets, proper family relations and hygiene, man could attain a level of right standing or *'righteousness'* before the Lord God. In Leviticus we learn that along with these religious practices, the people of God were to be circumspect in their personal, moral, and social living, which was a direct contrast to the current practices of the pagan nations around them. One prominent religious ceremony mentioned in Leviticus was the yearly practiced *"Day of Atonement,"* which was a special way of honoring God and being cleansed from sin. The book of Leviticus also gives us specific instructions on how the actual sacrifices and offerings were to be used, and how the high priest, the priests and people should conduct themselves during these rituals. All in all, this book is about the holiness of God and the ways his people can enter into a relationship with him. To the Christian, all these rituals and instructions were met through the life, death and resurrection of Jesus Christ, so for us there is no need for these rules and rituals.

NOTABLE VERSES

Leviticus 1:4

" And he shall put his hand upon the head of the burnt offering; and it shall be accepted for him to make atonement for him."

Sacrifices and offerings were a way of forgiving ones sins before God at this time, today we have Christ and the Cross, Amen!

Leviticus 17:11

" For the life of the flesh is in the blood: and I have given it to you upon the altar to make an atonement for your souls: for it is the blood that makes an atonement for the soul."

Here, we recognize the holiness of blood. In the eyes of God, blood is a sacred thing, whether in men, women or animals, so we should always try to honor it.

Leviticus 19:18

" You shall not avenge, nor bear any grudge against the children of your people, but you shall love your neighbor as yourself: I am the LORD."

Here, we see a famous teaching of Christ, long before He entered the world. Love for your neighbor is a goal we should all strive for, and in doing so we will please our Creator!

Leviticus 25:19

"And all of you shall honor the fiftieth year, and proclaim liberty throughout all the land unto all the inhabitants thereof: it shall be a jubilee unto you; and all of you shall return possessions to every man which is his, and all of you shall return every slave unto his family."

The Jubilee year was an exciting time of rejoicing in Israel! It happened every fifty years in ancient Israel.

A Levite Priest in the Old Testament

Numbers

$\int$

Author and Date   Moses was the author of the book of Numbers, this book was written around 1400 B.C. The word Numbers in this case more resembles a *"Census"* or numbering of the people of Israel. The significance of the book of Numbers is essential to us because it gives the historical and spiritual timeframe between the Israelites receiving the law in Exodus and Leviticus, and preparing them to enter the Promised Land.

Synopsis   The storyline of the book of Numbers takes place in the wilderness during the years of the wanderings of the Israelites from Egypt to Canaan, the *'land of promise.'* The first part of the book gives the events of the first generation of Israel journeying through the wilderness, while the rest of the book gives us the experiences of the next generation of Israelites. Rebellion happens regularly by the newly freed Israelites that followed Moses into the desert, and consequently judgment comes to them! However, the next generation of Israelites obeys the Lord God and blessing follows this generation of Israelites. The basic story throughout this time is as follows; God reveals Himself to Moses and the children of Israel, they obey and are always blessed, but when they do not obey they are cursed! The Israelites needed much instruction at this time before they could enter into the *'promised land,'* for they had spent almost 400 years of captivity in Egypt, and had forgotten the ways of the Lord. This is why it is so difficult for the first generation of Israelites to succeed in the things of God. So we learn in Numbers it was actually the 2nd generation of Israelites that were faithful to the ways of God, and finally did enter the Promised Land in Canaan. Interestingly, the book of Numbers is important to Christians because it is mentioned several times in the New Testament, it is a warning to us, as it refers to the first group of Israelites out of Egypt and how they often acted wrongly during their time of trial and testing. We must always remember that the Lord

God is a God of love, but He is also holy! This is the main message of the book of Numbers. At the end of the book, we see the 2nd generation of Israelites inheriting the '*promised land*' as God promised.

NOTABLE VERSES
Numbers 6:24-26
"The LORD bless you and keep you; the LORD make his face shine upon you and be gracious to you; the LORD turns his face toward you and give you peace."
In this verse, we see an ancient Hebrew blessing given by the priests to the people. It gives those who hear it great comfort and encouragement whenever it is said, for it reminds those who have faith in the Lord God they can easily receive His favor.

Numbers 11:23
"And the LORD said unto Moses, Is the LORD's hand waxed short? You shall see now whether my word shall come to pass unto you or not."
When God promises something to you, it will come to pass for He is God Almighty. What we must do is stand on the promises and wait until the proper time for it to manifest.

Deuteronomy

§

Author and date   Moses was the author of the book of Deuteronomy, he wrote it around 1400 B.C. The word "Deuteronomy" literally means second law, it comes from the Greek words *Nomos* (law) and *Deutero* (second). In the book of Deuteronomy, Moses is essentially preaching to the Israelites or restating the Law to a new generation of Israelites who had arisen during the 40 years in the wilderness.

Synopsis   The Israelites were about to enter the *'promised land'* given to them by God. This group of people was mostly made up of the descendants of Israel who did not receive God's judgment against them in the wilderness. When they were about to enter the Promised Land in Canaan they needed to be reminded of the laws of God and their standing with Him. In Deuteronomy the Israelites were commanded to remember four basic things, they were; *God's faithfulness, God's holiness, God's blessings, and God's warnings.* As we study Deuteronomy we see the first three chapters recapping the trip from Egypt to their current location, which was an area called Moab, after this in Chapter four the Israelites are called to obedience, to be faithful to the God who just delivered them from their bondage in Egypt. From Chapters five to twenty-six there is a reminding of the *'Laws of God,'* and an in-depth meaning of them, which included the *'Ten Commandments,'* and the laws concerning sacrifices and specials days. In Deuteronomy we learn blessings are always promised to those who obey, and curses and judgment are promised to those who break the law. The subject of blessing and cursing is continued in the rest of chapters until the end of the book. In this book we also see a part of the nature of the Lord being revealed, and it is the people of God who are always given a choice, and the choice is always obvious, which is either obey and serve the true and living God and receive his blessings or reject his ways and trouble comes. This is rightly the primary teaching throughout this book. At the end of the book, we see Moses encouraging Israel to be faithful to the Lord, and anointing Joshua to be the new leader of Israel. After this Moses gives his farewell blessing to the tribes of Israel and then dies in sight of the Promised Land!

NOTABLE VERSES:

Deuteronomy 4:2
"All of you shall not add unto the word which I command you, neither shall all you diminish from it, that all of you may keep the commandments of the LORD your God which I command you."
Here, we see in this scripture how beneficial it is to remain faithful to what scriptures say, and not add or subtract to them. This is important to remaining faithful to God.

Deuteronomy 6:4-7
"Hear, O Israel: The LORD our God is one LORD: And you shall love the LORD your God with all of your heart, and with all your soul, and with all your might. And these words, which I command you this day, shall be in your heart: And you shall teach them diligently unto your children, and shall talk of them when you sit in your house, and when you walk by the way, and when you lie down, and when you rise up."
In this verse, we see the most valuable command in the entire Bible, which is to love the Lord God, this is not that difficult to do, for once you get to know him you find out how wonderful He is.

Deuteronomy 8
"Know then in your heart that as a man disciplines his son, so the Lord your God disciplines you."
Here, we understand the father and son relationship God wants to have with us, and if we let him, God will be the best Father we could ever imagine.

Deuteronomy 10:14
"Behold, the heaven and the heaven of heavens is the LORD's your God, the earth also, with all that therein is."
Here, we see once again that God Almighty owns and encompasses everything! All things both in heaven and earth.

Deuteronomy 28:3
"You will be blessed in the city and blessed in the country"
In this verse, we can see that God blessings are for us everywhere we go in life! In ancient times people served many false gods, there was a god of the ocean and a god of the land and a god of fertility, and so on, but in the Lord God we learn that He is the God of everything.

Deuteronomy 30:15-16
"See, I have set before you this day life and good, and death and evil; In that I command you this day to love the LORD your God, to walk in his ways, and to keep his commandments and his statutes and his judgments, that you may live and multiply: and the LORD your God shall bless you in the land where you go to possess. See, I set before you today life and prosperity, or death and destruction."
God always gives man the opportunity to choose how we will live. If we choose to obey God and embrace his ways, tremendous blessing will come into our lives! In this verse of scripture we see that life and prosperity are God's ultimate will for mankind. Often we see many religious people proclaim death and destruction as the foundation of their religion but this is contrary to the perfect will of God.

Moses anoints Joshua as the new leader of Israel before they enter the Promised Land. Joshua was the best successor to Moses because he served under him for many years.

Joshua

§

Author and Date   The book of Joshua was likely written between 1400 and 1370 B.C.by the warrior, Joshua son of Nun. The name Joshua means *"the Lord is Salvation."* He was the successor of Moses as the new leader and general over Israel as they entered the Promised Land. Due to the death of Joshua the end of the book was written by someone else.

Synopsis   The book of Joshua gives us an overview of the military expeditions of the nation of Israel in conquering the land of Canaan, which was the land promised to them by the Lord. As we learned earlier, when the *'Exodus'* from Egypt was completed, many people of Israel sinned greatly against God and therefore spent forty years in the wilderness as their judgment. After this, there was a new generation of Israelites who would actually enter the Promised Land, but to do this they first had to conquer the peoples of these territories. The book of Joshua gives us many details about these battles and how the land was eventually conquered, and divided among the tribes of Israel. It took the people of Israel about 20 years under Joshua's leadership to conquer the land of Canaan, the land of promise.

NOTABLE VERSES
Joshua 1:6-9
"Be strong and courageous, because you will lead these people to inherit the land I swore to their forefathers to give them. Be strong and very courageous. Be careful to obey all the law my servant Moses gave you; do not turn from it to the right or to the left, that you may be successful wherever you go. Do not let this Book of the Law depart from your mouth; meditate on it day and night, so that you may be careful to do everything written in it. Then you will be prosperous and successful. Have I not

commanded you? Be strong and courageous. Do not be terrified; do not be discouraged, for the LORD your God will be with you wherever you go."

We recognize the importance of being strong and courageous in our faith, both in obeying his laws and exercising our faith in Him. When we do this, blessing and prosperity is ours.

Joshua 24:14-18

" Now therefore fear the LORD, and serve him in sincerity and in truth: and put away the gods which your fathers served on the other side of the water, and in Egypt; and serve all of you the LORD. And if it seems evil unto you to serve the LORD, choose you this day whom you will serve; whether the gods which your fathers served that were on the other side of the flood, or the gods of the Amorites, in whose land all of you dwell: but as for me and my house, we will serve the LORD. And the people answered and said, God forbid that we should forsake the LORD, to serve other gods. For the LORD our God, he it is that brought us up and our fathers out of the land of Egypt, from the house of bondage, and did those great signs in our sight, and preserved us in all the way we went, and among all the peoples through whom we passed: And the LORD drove out from before us all the people, even the Amorites which dwelt in the land: therefore will we also serve the LORD; for he is our God."

Now we see an exhortation to serve God in faithfulness. We do this by honoring Him in all our ways and keeping Him first place in our lives above all the falsehoods of the day. The fear of the Lord is the beginning of all wisdom, but fear based in love.

Judges

§

Author and Date   The book of Judges was probably written between 1045 and 1000 B.C. by the prophet Samuel, but we do not know.

Synopsis   The book of Judges is about the time frame from the death of Joshua until the time of the monarch kings of Israel. Initially, the children of Israel at this time had rulers or '*Judges*' leading them. Some of the prominent judges were people like Deborah the warrior Jewess, Gideon, Jephthah and the mighty Samson. The storyline in Judges is how the people of Israel often abandoned the Lord their God, and as they abandoned God they suffered great defeat at the hands of their enemies, but even in their disobedience God always was willing to forgive and bless them if they turned back to Him. Interestingly, in Judges we learn that when the Israelites turned their backs on the Lord, they often served and worshiped the two detestable gods of the ancient world called '*Baal*' and '*Ashtoreth*,' who were the false deities of their neighbors, the Philistines and Canaanites. Throughout the book of Judges when we do see the Israelites begin to suffer and experience judgment, they would often cry out to the Lord and He would always bless them, usually by sending a righteous ruler or '*Judge*' who would lead them to deliverance. The cycle of rebellion against God, and then repentance often continued throughout this time in Israel's history. The main reason why God would bless Israel and never utterly forsake them was because of the covenant He swore to the patriarch Abraham, the father of the Jewish people. God's mercy was significant at this time, for it extended for a period in Israel's history that spanned almost 500 years.

NOTABLE VERSES
Judges 2:16-19
"Then the LORD raised up judges, who saved them out of the hands of these raiders. Yet they would not listen to their judges but prostituted themselves to other gods and worshiped them. Unlike their fathers, they quickly turned from the way in which their fathers had walked, the way of obedience to the LORD's commands. Whenever the LORD rose up a judge for them, he was with the judge and saved them out of the hands of their enemies as long as the judge lived; for the LORD had compassion on them as they groaned under those who oppressed and afflicted them. But when the judge died, the people returned to ways even more corrupt than those of their fathers, following other gods and serving and worshiping them. They refused to give up their evil practices and stubborn ways."

Now we see the mentality of the people at this time, what is intriguing is the mercy of the Lord towards them. This was before Christ and the Cross, so sin was dealt with in man quite differently than it is now. The people of God at that time did not have the indwelling *'Spirit of God'* to help them live good lives as we do, so this was one reason why God was always merciful to them. Today however, we have been given the power of the Holy Spirit, so there is certainly no excuse to sin in the way the ancients Israelites did.

Ruth

§

Author and Date   We do not know the author of the book of Ruth, but some scholars believe this book was written by the Prophet Samuel. The name Ruth means *"friend,"* and in the text of the book of Ruth we learn that she was not only a daughter-in- law but also a loyal friend to Naomi, the Jewess. The book was probably written sometime between 1011 and 931 B.C.

Synopsis   The book of Ruth is about love, redemption and the decisions that one must make in life because of circumstances. This book shows us that regardless of what happens in life, we can live good lives before the Lord. The book of Ruth also shows if we trust in God we will experience great blessing in our lives, as will our descendants. Ruth begins in a country called Moab, which was a pagan nation situated north of Israel, and from there swiftly moved to the outskirts of the city of Bethlehem, where both King David and Jesus Christ were born. The initial storyline of the book tells us about a drought and famine occurring during this time which causes a man named Elimelech and his wife Naomi to move from Israel to Moab. However, soon after they arrive in Moab, Elimelech dies and Naomi is left with her two sons, who soon marry two Moabite girls named Orpah and Ruth. Unfortunately, later in the story we learn both of the sons die, and Naomi is left alone with Orpah and Ruth in this strange land, so now decisions had to be made. Orpah returns to her Moabite parents, but Ruth decides to stay with Naomi, wherever she goes. Naomi the Jewess decides to move back to her hometown Bethlehem with Ruth in tow, and as they return to her hometown they are essentially destitute, but through Divine circumstance the young Ruth marries a wealthy Israelite named Boaz. They soon have a son named Obed who becomes the grandfather of the revered King David. In David and his lineage, the Messiah, Jesus Christ is revealed to the world!

Notable Verses
Ruth 1:16-17
" And Ruth said, Implore me not to leave you, or to return from following after you: for where you go, I will go; and where you lodge, I will lodge: your people shall be my people, and your God my God: Where you die, I will die, and there will I be buried."

In this famous verse, we learn that whatever our position is in life if we trust in God and embrace his ways good things will be in store for us. In this case, the unbelieving Ruth becomes a wealthy and loved woman, and a person who had the privilege of being the great grandmother of a famous King.

Ruth 4: 21-22
"And Salmon brings forth Boaz, and Boaz brings forth Obed, And Obed brings forth Jesse, and Jesse brings forth David."

Now we see the famous lineage of Ruth the Moabite, who was a foreigner to the promises of the Lord God. God sometimes uses people outside his holy covenant.

Ruth the Moabite gleans wheat from the land of the Israelite
Boaz, who would become her future husband. The story of Ruth
and Boaz is one of the great love stories of the Bible.

1ˢᵗ Samuel

§

Author and Date The author of 1st Samuel is unknown, but most scholars believe the prophet Samuel wrote part of the book. The name means *"heard by God,"* and through scripture we learn that Samuel was born because God heard the prayer of his mother. The events of 1st Samuel occurred during a 100 year period, from around 1100 B.C. to 1000 B.C. The events of 2nd Samuel cover another 40 years. The date of the writing would be sometime after 960 B.C.

Synopsis First Samuel is about the establishment of the rule of kings in the history of Israel around 1000 B.C. The prophet Samuel is considered the final judge in this era. The book of 1st Samuel initially tells us about the life and times of Samuel the prophet, and then goes on to Saul, who was Israel's first King, and then to the mighty King David. The book of Samuel begins with the birth and early life of the prophet Samuel, and his faithfulness to the Lord during a corrupt time in Israel's history. During this time in Israel's history, the Philistines were one of the chief enemies of the nation, often at war with Israel, and even at one point taking the *'Ark of the Covenant,'* the most prominent symbol and treasure of Israel. However, it eventually was returned to Israel because of the Lord's wrath against them. The scenario of Israel at this time was always the same, when Israel stood upright before the Lord, all was well with them, but when they sinned and fell away from God they suffered substantial loss. We also learn at this time Israel demanded that God give them a flesh and blood King to lead them like other nations, but this demand from the Israelites displeased the Lord immensely because He wanted to be their one and only King, forever. So Saul, from the tribe of Benjamin is chosen and anointed by the prophet Samuel as Israel's first King.

Saul is popular and successful at first, but towards the end of his reign he becomes arrogant and spiritually corrupt, even consulting with a pagan witch for guidance, which was strictly forbidden for any Israelite to do. After Saul's apostasy, the Lord then leads the prophet Samuel to the young shepherd boy David son of Jesse, and anoints him to be ruler over Israel. In the course of time, David strikes down the notorious Goliath, marries one of Saul's daughters, befriends Saul's favorite son Jonathan, and becomes a national hero. This leads to great jealousy by King Saul, even as he attempts to take David's life. Saul eventually dies a broken and confused man along with his sons, and David becomes King of Israel according to the prophecy given by Samuel.

NOTABLE VERSES

1 Samuel 8:6-7
"But the thing displeased Samuel, when they said, 'Give us a king to rule over us.' And Samuel prayed unto the LORD. And the LORD said unto Samuel, hearken unto the voice of the people in all that they say unto you: for they have not rejected you, but they have rejected me, that I should not reign over them."
This is certainly a momentous verse because it shows the Lord's heart and his desire to be the undeniable sovereign leader in Israel, but the people wanted a flesh and blood leader other than God.

1 Samuel 15:22-23
"And Samuel said, does the LORD have great delight in burnt offerings and sacrifices, as in obeying the voice of the LORD? Behold, to obey is better than sacrifice! and to hearken to Him is better than the fat of rams. For rebellion is as the sin of witchcraft, and stubbornness is as iniquity and idolatry. Because you have rejected the word of the LORD, he has also rejected you from being king."
In this verse, we understand that *'faith in God'* is so much more beneficial than religious acts. To hear God's *'Word'* and obey what He says is the most valuable thing we can do to please the God of the universe!

The young David kills the Philistine Goliath

2nd Samuel

§

Author and Date   The author of the book of 2nd Samuel is unknown, but it was written sometime after 960 B.C.

Synopsis   The book of 2nd Samuel is mostly about the life and times of King David and the history of Israel around 1000 B.C. The book of 2nd Samuel gives us David's successes and failures as Israel's most famous King. The book starts off with the death of Saul and Jonathan, and then moves to the warrior/poet David as he is crowned king over Judah and Israel. When David's reign comes into fruition, he moves the capitol to Jerusalem. Notably, because of this act 3000 years ago the Jews of today still believe that the city of Jerusalem is their rightful capitol. As David reigns in Jerusalem as Israel's king, he receives magnificent promises and blessings from the Lord. The primary blessing is the prophecy given to him that his descendants would reign forever, and God's blessing would never leave him or his people. We also see David as the military commander of Israel. At this historic time he leads the nation to many victories, which gives expansion to the territory of Israel. In one of the most memorable stories in the Bible we read the full tale of David's act of adultery with Bathsheba, and the murder of her husband Uriah the Hittite. Because of this act, and other rebellion God's judgment comes on David and his ruling family. The results from this are the kingdom of Israel experiences war, murder, rape and famine.

NOTABLE VERSES
2 Samuel 7:16
"Your house and your kingdom will endure forever before me; your throne will be established forever."

In this verse we see the blessing of God coming to David and his descendants forever! We also see this as a prophecy about Jesus Christ and His reign as '*King of Kings*' to all believers.

2 Samuel 22:17
"He reached down from on high and took hold of me; he drew me out of the deep waters."
We see that God can reach us anywhere we are, and take us to a better place in our lives! God is always near, ready, willing and able to help us in our time of need, He did this several times throughout the life of David.

2 Samuel 22:25
"Therefore the Lord has rewarded me according to my righteousness, according to my cleanness in his sight."
Here, we see that God often rewards us on how we act in this life. If we do the right things we will be rewarded for our actions, but God rewards us in His way, and in His time.

The Ark of the Covenant was the most influential religious object in ancient Israel. The mystery of what happened to the Ark is still a great question to all.

1ˢᵗ Kings

§

Author and Date   We do not know the author of the book of 1st Kings, but tradition tells us it was written by the prophet Jeremiah. The book of 1st Kings was likely written between 560 and 540 B.C.

Synopsis   This book is primarily about the history of the monarchies of Israel and Judah, and the ministry of Elijah, who was a significant Jewish prophet. The book begins with Solomon, the son of King David, and his ascent to becoming King of Israel. At this time the nation of Israel moves from a united Kingdom to one which separates into two, Judah and Israel. Solomon was the son of David and Bathsheba, who had a special anointing on him throughout his life. Solomon at the beginning of his reign accomplished much and was an extremely faithful servant of the Lord, but later in his life he sinned greatly. Although he built the Lord's temple, which was his greatest accomplishment, later in life he was drawn away from his relationship to the Lord by marrying foreign wives who persuaded him to worship foreign gods. After Solomon died, the nation of Israel was ruled by several kings who were not faithful to the Lord God. Two of the unfaithful rulers were named Ahab and Jezebel (Jezebel was his wife), these two encouraged the people of Israel to worship and serve the detestable god named *"Baal"* (Baal was the god of the Canaanites, who was Israel's next door neighbor). In one of the most dramatic stories in this book we see the famed Israelite prophet Elijah confronting the Canaanite believers and their priests over their pagan god and practices. In this confrontation he prayed that the God of Israel would appear and do the miraculous, and defeat them, and of course, God did. Elijah throughout this book tried to turn the Israelites back to the worship of Jehovah, the true and living God.

NOTABLE VERSES

1 Kings 3:7-10

" And now, O LORD my God, you have made your servant king instead of David my father: and I am but a little child: I know not how to go out or come in. And your servant is in the midst of your people which you have chosen, a great people, that cannot be numbered nor counted for multitude. Give therefore your servant an understanding heart to judge your people, that I may discern between good and bad: for who is able to judge this your so great a people? And the prayer pleased the LORD, that Solomon had asked this thing."

We have the young Solomon becoming King of Israel and knowing it was a tough job he asks God for wisdom. Wisdom is something that we all need in our life, so Solomon gives us an excellent example to follow. This request pleased God, so God not only gave him immense wisdom, but wealth and power, as well.

1 Kings 9:3-5

"And the LORD said unto him, I have heard your prayer and your supplication, that you have made before me: I have consecrated this house, which you have built, to put my name there forever; and mine eyes and mine heart shall be there perpetually. And if you will walk before me, as David your father walked, in integrity of heart, and in uprightness, to do according to all that I have commanded you, and will keep my statutes and my judgments: Then I will establish the throne of your kingdom upon Israel for ever, as I promised to David your father, saying, There shall not fail you a man upon the throne of Israel."

When the long awaited *'Temple of the Lord'* was built by Solomon, God was pleased with the effort and gave his blessing upon it.

1 Kings 10:23

"King Solomon was greater in riches and wisdom that all the other Kings of the earth. The whole world sought audience with him to hear the wisdom God had put in his heart."

Here, we have the blessing of the Lord upon Solomon and his reign. This is a superb example to us, for if we put God and His Kingdom first in our lives, the blessing of prosperity will flow to us, but more beneficial than prosperity is wisdom, the wisdom that comes from God himself.

1 Kings 17:1
"Now Elijah the Tishbite, from Tishbe in Gilead, said to Ahab, 'As the LORD, and the God of Israel, lives, whom I serve, and there will be neither dew nor rain in the next few years except at my word.'"

In those days prophets like Elijah had tremendous power and authority before both God and the people.

2nd Kings

§

Author and Date   The tradition is the prophet Jeremiah was the author of 2nd Kings. The book of 2nd Kings, along with 1st Kings was likely written between 560 and 540 B.C. It continues the story of the Jewish kings over the divided kingdom (Israel and Judah). The book of 2nd Kings concludes with the final overthrow and deportation of the people of Israel and Judah to Assyria and Babylon.

Synopsis   In 2nd Kings we see the prophets of God warn the people that judgment is coming to the northern and southern kingdoms of Israel and Judah, however, the people still do not repent. The main problem at this time was the leaders of Israel and Judah were wicked and led many people astray. During this time when the Kings remained faithful to the Lord, blessing would come to the nation, however more often than not they turned their backs on God. The two main prophets of this book are Elijah and Elisha, both of whom experienced many dramatic miracles that gave glory to God in the midst of the pagan peoples. However, even though these magnificent prophets performed miracles in front of the people, Israel and Judah did not repent at their preaching, so eventually the nation of Assyria destroyed Israel, and the Babylonians destroyed Judah. In the conclusion of understanding this book there are three distinct messages to be learned; first of all, the Lord will judge his people when they disobey and turn their backs on Him. Secondly, the word of the true prophets of God always comes to pass, and thirdly, the Lord is always faithful. God always remembers His promises and covenants, even in despite of the disobedience of the people and the kings who ruled over them. God always will bless his people if they turn to Him.

NOTABLE VERSES

2Kings5:13

"Naaman's servants went to him and said, "My father if the prophet has told you to do some great thing, would you have not done it? How much more, then, when he tells you, wash and be cleansed"! So he went down and dipped himself in the Jordan River seven times as the man had told him, and his flesh was restored and became clean like that of a young boy."

In this story we see the importance of obeying the Lord and his 'Word,' which always brings victory in our lives.

2Kings 7:1-2

Elisha said. "Hear the Word of the Lord. This is what the Lord says: About this time tomorrow, a seah of flour will sell for shekel and two seahs of barley for a shekel at the gate of Samaria," and the officer on whose arm the king was leaning said to the man of God, "Look even if the Lord should open the floodgates of Heaven could this happen? "You will see it with your own eyes, answered Elisha, "but you will not eat any of it"

When God's miracles come, they come in abundance, for we need only to believe. As we see once again the sovereignty of the Lord over the natural world. Interestingly, we see the person who did not believe did not receive any reward!

2Kings 17:7-8

"All this took place because the Israelites had sinned against the LORD their God, who had brought them up out of Egypt from under the power of Pharaoh King of Egypt. They worshiped other gods and followed the practices of the nations the LORD had driven out before them, as well as the practices that the kings of Israel had introduced."

Here we wonder why the Israelites would turn from the God who delivered them out of their bondage and gave them so many miracles. Unfortunately this occurred often in history of the Israelites. It probably had to do with them not be grounded in the *'Word'* and their true faith. The worship of pagan gods and deities by mankind was common during this era of time.

2 Kings 22:1-2
"Josiah was eight years old when he became king, and he reigned in Jerusalem thirty-one years. He did what was right in the eyes of the LORD and walked in all the ways of his father David, not turning aside to the right or to the left."
Even at a young age we can serve the Lord and know Him and his ways. If we do this in our youth it brings great blessing later in life.

1ˢᵗ Chronicles

§

Author and Date   The writer of the book of 1ˢᵗ Chronicles is not known, but many believe it was written by the prophet Ezra, and was likely written between 450 and 425 B.C.

Synopsis   The book of Chronicles covers mostly the same information as 1st and 2nd Samuel and1st & 2nd Kings. This book was written for the Jewish exiles to help those returning to Israel understand how to worship God, and remind them of their magnificent heritage in the Lord. The beginning chapters of the book are dedicated to lists and genealogies, from the beginning of recorded Scripture to the time of King Saul. However, overwhelmingly the book of 1st Chronicles gives us a good synopsis of the life and times of the revered King David. It also gives us a history lesson about the returning exiles from the Babylonian captivity. This book ends with the death of David, and Solomon becoming the new King of Israel.

NOTABLE VERSES
1 Chronicles 16:8-17
"David delivered first this psalm to thank the LORD into the hand of Asaph and his brethren. Give thanks unto the LORD, call upon his name, make known his deeds among the people. Sing unto him, sing psalms unto him, talk of all his wondrous works. Glory in his holy name: let the heart of them rejoice that seek the LORD. Seek the LORD and his strength, seek his face continually. Remember his marvelous works that he has done, his wonders, and the judgments of his mouth, you seed of Israel his servant, you children of Jacob, his chosen ones. He is the LORD our God; his judgments are in all the earth. Be mindful always of his covenant; the word which he commanded to a thousand generations; Even of the covenant which

be made with Abraham, and of his oath unto Isaac; And has confirmed the same to Jacob for a law, and to Israel for an everlasting covenant."

We see the psalmist David speaking about the great covenant God gave to the people of Israel through Abraham, also is given the knowledge that it is always good to remind ourselves of the promises of God in our lives through praise and worship!

1 Chronicles 29:11

"Yours, O LORD, is the greatness and the power and the glory and the majesty and the splendor, for everything in heaven and earth is yours. Yours, O LORD, is the kingdom; you are exalted as head over all."

This is a significant exhortation to the reality that the Lord God is the greatest power and authority in all of heaven and earth, and the reality that those who acknowledge Him can live in His power and authority.

2ⁿᵈ Chronicles

§

Author and Date   The author of the book of 2ⁿᵈ Chronicles is not known, but many believe was written by Ezra. The book of 2ⁿᵈ Chronicles was likely written between 450 and 425 B.C.

Synopsis   The books of 1st and 2nd Chronicles mostly covers the same information as 1ˢᵗ and 2ⁿᵈ Samuel and 1ˢᵗ and 2ⁿᵈ Kings. The book gives us added insight into Israel's religious history. The book also gives us the history of the Kingdom of Judah, from the time of Solomon's reign to Israel's Babylonian exile. The decline of Judah is disappointing, but emphasis is given to the spiritual reformers who zealously seek to turn the people back to God. In this book, little is said about the bad kings of this time, but much is said about the good kings and their accomplishments. The end of this book is most notable to the reader because it is during this time the Lord God brings King Nebuchadnezzar and his Babylonian army against Jerusalem. When they come to Jerusalem, the Temple is destroyed and the people are taken into bondage.

NOTABLE VERSES
2 Chronicles 2:1
"Solomon gave orders to build a temple for the Name of the LORD and a royal palace for himself."
Solomon is not only known for his marvelous wisdom, but his extensive building projects. The building of the *'Temple of the Lord'* was his most celebrated work.

2 Chronicles 29:1-3

"Hezekiah was twenty-five years old when he became king, and he reigned in Jerusalem twenty-nine years. His mother's name was Abijah daughter of Zechariah. He did what was right in the eyes of the LORD, just as his father David had done. In the first month of the first year of his reign, he opened the doors of the temple of the LORD and repaired them."

King Hezekiah was one of the good Kings of Israel. He received blessing in his reign because he remained faithful to the Lord and his laws. In this verse we also see the first thing Hezekiah did when he became king was to repair the Temple of Solomon, showing God and all the people that the Lord was first in his life. In these acts we learn blessings always come when we put God first place in our lives.

2 Chronicles 36:23

"This is what Cyrus king of Persia says: 'The LORD, the God of heaven, has given me all the kingdoms of the earth and has appointed me to build a temple for him at Jerusalem in Judah. Anyone of his people among you—may the LORD his God be with him, and let him go up."

Here we learn that even pagan kings indirectly serve the Lord God and do his will. This is an extremely fascinating insight into God's sovereignty.

Ezra

§

Author and Date   The author of the book of Ezra was the Jewish prophet Ezra. The name means "*Help*," and was likely written between 460 and 440 B.C.

Synopsis   The book of Ezra is about the people of Israel when they returned to the land after the Babylonian captivity beginning around 538 B.C. It is also about the rebuilding of the *'Temple of Solomon'* in Jerusalem. The book of Ezra covers the time frame concerning the return from captivity, to the rebuilding of the *'Temple'* and the decree of Artaxerxes, the king of Persia. The beginning of the book tells us about the first return under the prophet Zerubbabel, the re-building of the *'Temple,'* and the ministry of Ezra. Interestingly, since well over half a century elapsed between some of the chapters, the characters of the first part of the book had died by the time Ezra began his ministry in Jerusalem. Ezra the priest is prominent not only in the book of Ezra, but also in the book of Nehemiah.

Notable Verses
Ezra 1
"In the first year of Cyrus king of Persia, in order to fulfill the word of the Lord spoken by Jeremiah, the Lord moved the heart of Cyrus king of Persia to make a proclamation throughout his realm and also to put it in writing."This is what Cyrus king of Persia says: "'The Lord, the God of heaven, has given me all the kingdoms of the earth and he has appointed me to build a temple for him at Jerusalem in Judah. Any of his people among you may go up to Jerusalem in Judah and build the temple of the Lord, the God of Israel, the God who is in Jerusalem. And may their God be with them. And in any locality where survivors may now be living, the

people are to provide them with silver and gold, with goods and livestock, and with freewill offerings for the temple of God in Jerusalem.'"

In this scripture we learn something interesting about the Lord God, He often uses non-believers in Him to accomplish his will and purposes in the earth. The Persians at this time in history were a pagan people but due to God's sovereign purposes a relationship with this king of Persia was developed. Prophetically, when Cyrus the king of Persia was in the first year of his reign, he was led by God to make a decree that the Jews should return to their land and rebuild the temple of Solomon to worship God. He allowed the Jews to take their sacred vessels and writings and even helped with the finances for this project.

Nehemiah

§

Author and Date   The author of the book of Nehemiah was the Israelite Ezra. The word Nehemiah means '*comfort of God*,' which is something we all need in this life. Interestingly, the books of Ezra and Nehemiah were once only one book, however this book was likely written between 445 and 420 B.C.

Synopsis   The book of Nehemiah is one of the history books of the Bible, it tells us the story of Israel's return from Babylonian captivity and the rebuilding of the Temple in Jerusalem.

Nehemiah was a Hebrew living in Persia when word reached him that the Temple in Jerusalem was being reconstructed. Nehemiah was concerned about this endeavor because he knew there was no wall to protect the city, so Nehemiah asked God to use him to help. God answered his prayer by softening the heart of the Persian king, a man named Artaxerxes, who gave him his blessing and permission to return to Jerusalem. In spite of much opposition, the wall around Jerusalem was built, and the people were inspired by Nehemiah's preaching. They gave money, supplies and man-power to complete the wall in a remarkable 52 days. Soon after this, Nehemiah leaves Jerusalem. And after 12 years he returns to find the walls strong, but the people apostate, so he begins the work of teaching the people morality and righteousness. He does it with considerable authority and power, even putting curses on some un-ruly people, and pulling out the hair of some apostate Jews. This type of preaching must have prevailed because he re-establishes true worship, prayer and adherence to the Word of God.

NOTABLE VERSES

Nehemiah 1:3

"Those who survived the exile and are back in the province are in great trouble and disgrace. The wall of Jerusalem is broken down, and its gates have been burned with fire."

The nation of Israel was in shambles. Nehemiah steps in to help and does an amazing job helping to re-build Jerusalem. This is the attitude God's people should have, to always be available to serve, wherever needed.

Nehemiah 1:11

"O Lord, let your ear be attentive to the prayer of this your servant and to the prayer of your servants who delight in revering your name. Give your servant success today by granting him favor in the presence of this man."

The prophet Nehemiah is asking God for favor in his endeavor. If we approach God with a good heart and ask Him for something, He will grant the request. The interesting thing here is how Nehemiah mentions to reverence the name of the Lord! This is important when we approach God in prayer.

The Israelites re-build the Jerusalem Temple around 538 B.C.

Esther

§

Author and Date   We do not know the author of Esther, but some believe it may have been Mordacai, who is one of the main characters in this book. The Persian name *"Esther"* more than likely means *"Star,"* the Hebrew name is *"Hadassah"* which means *"Myrtle tree,"* this book was likely written between 460 and 350 B.C.

Synopsis   The book of Esther is set in the ancient city of Susa, the capitol of Persia, during the reign of King Xerxes around 480 B.C. The main lesson we learn in this book is the sovereignty of the Lord God. Although written about the children of Israel, all believers can rejoice and know that our God rules and reigns over all the nations on the earth. We learn about Jewish history, as the *'Feast of Purim'* is started. The holiday of *Purim* is about the deliverance of the Jewish people brought about by God through the Jewish woman Esther. The book can be divided into four important parts; In the first part, Esther replaces Queen Vashti of Persia, in the second part, the Israelite Mordecai overcomes one of King Xerxes chief advisors, a man named Haman, in the third part, the Jews survive Haman's attempt to destroy them and in the fourth part, great blessings come to the Jews living in exile. The main theme of this book is about a Jewish woman who is essentially a slave in a foreign land, becoming queen of the country where she resides. This is somewhat similar to the story of Joseph in the book of Genesis. The most dramatic part of this story is when Esther, the queen, becomes aware of a plot to destroy the Jewish people living in Persia, and with the help of her uncle named Mordacai, she willingly does what she can to destroy the intentions of the man behind this plot who is named Haman. Haman happens to be the Kings top advisor. In this story risking her life Esther proves to be a worthy leader of the Jewish people. Haman's plans to destroy the Jews eventually ends up with his own demise, and the Jewish people are saved from destruction.

NOTABLE VERSES
Esther 2:15
"Now when the time came for Esther to go to the king, she asked for nothing other than what Hegai, the king's eunuch who was in charge of the harem, suggested."
We understand the importance of gaining wisdom from people who are experts in the matters we experience in life.

Esther 6:12
"Since Mordecai, before whom your downfall has begun, is of Jewish origin, you cannot stand against him - you will surely come to ruin."
The Lord's covenant with the Jewish people was active at this time, so those who knew God and his oath to the children of Israel became indestructible.

The beautiful Jewish girl Esther becomes Queen of Persia

Job

§

Author and Date   The author of the book of Job may have been Job himself, but we do not know. The date of the writing of the book of Job is also not clear to us, but many believe it is the one of the oldest books in the Bible. Job is believed by some scholars to be a non-Israelite living before the time of the Patriarchs. The name Job means *"one who is hated,"* which is intriguing because it seems Satan himself hated this man.

Synopsis   The book of Job begins with Satan, the rebellious angel, accusing righteous Job before God. Satan asserts that Job only serves and loves God because the Lord protects and blesses him. God does not agree with this accusation, but while still questioning God, Satan asks permission to test Job's faith and love for God. God agrees to this request, but with certain stipulations, so with this license Satan begins to destroy Job's life. The righteous Job loses his family, his wealth, his health and his standing in the community as Satan uses everything at his disposal to destroy him. Satan even tries to get him to curse God and die, but heroically Job remains faithful to God. During this onslaught from Satan, Job runs into three of his friends, Eliphaz, Bildad and Zophar. These three friends do not understand what has happened to their noble friend Job but gives him many answers as to why this is happening in his life, however, the answers the three friends give are all false. Throughout the book, Job endures his troubles and remains faithful to the Lord but begins to question God about what is happening in his life. And after much questioning the righteous Job finally hears from God, and is soon humiliated by the responses from the Lord. At the end of his questioning of God, Job realizes the Lord is sovereign over all people, nations and situations and comes to understand God's ways are just and true. At the end of the story, we see Job blessed abundantly by God and is restored to health, peace and prosperity.

NOTABLE VERSES

Job 1:1

"In the land of Uz there lived a man whose name was Job. This man was blameless and upright; he feared God and shunned evil."

The righteous Job is in a state of blessing in his life before Satan is allowed to destroy him. Notice how Job was a righteous man and did good but still suffering came upon him. This is a question man has asked throughout the ages.

Job 1:21

"Naked I came from my mother's womb, and naked I will depart. The LORD gave and the LORD has taken away; may the name of the LORD be praised."

In this famous verse we see the life cycle of man, the beginning and the end, and in both instances man has nothing, which should remind us of the shallowness of material things in life.

Job 38:1-2

"Then the LORD answered Job out of the Whirlwind. He said, 'Who is this that darkens my counsel with words without knowledge?'"

When unfortunate things happen to us in life, God usually gets the blame, but often the reason why trouble has come is unknown, so we should be like Job and always stay faithful.

In this picture we see one of the many trials of Job, as he is being questioned by his three friends who falsely accuse him of wrong doing before God. After his trials were over Job is restored and given considerable blessings.

The Psalms

§

Author and Date   The word Psalms means *"a song, hymn or prayer"* usually associated with an instrument. There were several writers of the book of Psalms, with King David being the main author of many of them. David's gifts as a writer and psalmist are evident in many of these psalms. Solomon, Moses, the sons of Korah, Asaph, Heman and Ethan are some of the other contributors to this great book. Because their were many writers associated with this book it took many years to compile. The oldest psalm is psalm 90 written by Moses and the most recent is psalm 13, which is a song of lament that was written during the Hebrews captivity by the Babylonians around 538 B.C. The book of Psalms may have taken almost 1000 years to bring into fruition.

Synopsis   The book of Psalms is the longest book in the Bible, the writings contained in this book can also be referred to as *"Praises"* or even *"Prayers."* There are about 150 individual Psalms in this book that refer to subjects like; God and His creation, war, worship, wisdom, sin and evil, judgment, justice, and the coming of the Messiah. The composition is a collection of prayers, poems and hymns that focus on the writer's thoughts on God through praise and adoration. Certain selections of this book were used as a hymnal in the worship services of the ancient Israelites.

Notable Verses
Psalm 19:1
"The heavens declare the glory of God; the skies proclaim the work of his hands."
Often the Psalms remind us of the glory and beauty of God in our natural world, even when we look up to the heavens our finite minds can reflect upon God's power and wonder.

Psalm 22:16-19
"Dogs have surrounded me; a band of evil men has encircled me, they have pierced my hands and my feet. I can count all my bones; people stare and gloat over me. They divide my garments among them and cast lots for my clothing."
Here, we have an outstanding prophecy about the crucifixion of Jesus Christ. King David prophesied about this event almost 1000 years before it happened.

Psalm 23:1
"The LORD is my shepherd, I shall not want."
In this famous psalm, we learn if God is our leader in life and we let Him guide us, we will never be in need.

Psalm 29:1-2
"Ascribe to the LORD, O mighty ones, ascribe to the LORD glory and strength. Ascribe to the LORD the glory due his name; worship the LORD in the splendor of his holiness."
Here we see a magnificent psalm for those who worship the Lord in spirit and truth, and honestly it is easy if we behold His glory.

Psalm 51:10
"Create in me a pure heart, O God, and renew a steadfast spirit within me."
God can always give us a new and bold spirit, all we have to do is ask.

Psalm 119:1-2
"Blessed are they whose ways are blameless, who walk according to the law of the LORD. Blessed are they who keep his statutes and seek him with all their heart."
In this promise we see that if we live our lives according to God's Word, enormous blessing will be ours.

The Proverbs

§

Author and Date   The word Proverbs means *"a popular, wise saying."* The writings in Proverbs were predominantly done by King Solomon. This book was compiled around 900 B.C. with the writings occurring during Solomon's reign as king of Israel. At this time in history due to God's blessing on the nation of Israel, the country's reputation soared, as did King Solomon's fame. During this time, many foreigners traveled considerable distances to hear the wisdom of this great King.

Synopsis   These writings are primarily about *'Wisdom.'* True wisdom is a gift from God giving someone the ability to see people, events, and circumstances in life with a divine perspective. In the book of Proverbs, Solomon gives us the *'gift of wisdom'* so we can address many situations in life. The topics include; personal issues, sexual relations, business, wealth, charity, ambition, discipline, debt, child-rearing, character, alcohol, politics, revenge, and godliness. The book of Proverbs is varied, there is no real story or particular person involved, and therefore, the voice of wisdom is the primary character. Wisdom is for everyone who has ever been born. This is why the book of Proverbs is so appealing, it is for everyone. Even though this book was written thousands of years ago we can still gain wisdom from the sayings and verses.

Notable Verses
Proverbs 1:7
"The fear of the LORD is the beginning of knowledge, but fools despise wisdom and knowledge."
This is a powerful verse for all. For to fear or give reverence to the Lord the creator of the universe is the wisest thing anyone can do in life.

The aged Solomon's words of wisdom still bless us today!

Proverbs 4:5
"Get wisdom, get understanding; do not forget my words or swerve from them."
The greatest wisdom anyone can gain in this life is not from a college or deep study of any subject, but from the *'Word of God,'* which is always true wisdom that lasts forever.

Proverbs 8:13-14

"To fear the LORD is to hate evil; I hate pride and arrogance, evil behavior and perverse speech. Counsel and sound judgment are mine; I have understanding and power."

We understand that when pride comes in a man's heart, so does arrogance, and with arrogance, evil behavior usually follows.

Ecclesiastes

§

Author and Date   The author of the book of Ecclesiastes is believed to be King Solomon. The word Ecclesiastes means *"One who speaks to an assembly"* or even *"Preacher."* This book was likely written towards the end of his reign as King of Israel around 935 B.C.

Synopsis   The book of Ecclesiastes primarily explores the issues of life through wisdom and perception. Solomon was one of the wisest, richest and most powerful Kings of the ancient world, and through his unique relationship with God he was allowed to deny himself nothing. As a writer, Solomon journeys through his life of excess but always keeps his faculties with him. As Solomon engaged in all forms of work and pleasure, he looked for meaning in it all, and found very little. At the end of the book, we see Solomon coming to the understanding that there is much meaninglessness in life except for a deep abiding faith in God. In discovering this truth Solomon tells the reader this should be the main pursuit of all men. Two words are repeated often in Ecclesiastes, the word *"vanity"* and *"meaningless."* These words are often used to emphasize the temporary nature of worldly pursuits, over eternal truths. The phrase *"under the sun"* occurs many times, which refers to life under heaven and all things on the earth. The first renderings of the book of Ecclesiastes describe all of the worldly things *"under the sun"* that the Preacher experiences. He tries science, wisdom and philosophy, pleasure of the body, materialism, mirth, alcohol, architecture, building, land acquisition, and the pursuit of a wealthy lifestyle. Towards the end of this book, the writer takes a philosophical look at life and comments on it. He comes to the conclusion that without God, there is no truth or meaning to life. He has experienced many things and realized that even the best of man's achievements are worth nothing in the scheme of all things, so he advises the reader to acknowledge God from youth, and serve Him.

Notable Verses

Ecclesiastes 1:18

"For with much wisdom comes much sorrow; the more knowledge, the more grief."
This is often a truth in life, the more we know about something often unhappiness follows.

Ecclesiastes 2:1-9

"Come now, I will test you with pleasure to find out what is good." But that also proved to be meaningless. "Laughter," I said, "is madness. And what does pleasure accomplish?" I tried cheering myself with wine, and embracing folly—my mind still guiding me with wisdom. I wanted to see what was good for people to do under the heavens during the few days of their lives. I undertook great projects: I built houses for myself and planted vineyards. I made gardens and parks and planted all kinds of fruit trees in them. ⁶ I made reservoirs to water groves of flourishing trees. I bought male and female slaves and had other slaves who were born in my house. I also owned more herds and flocks than anyone in Jerusalem before me. I amassed silver and gold for myself, and the treasure of kings and provinces. I acquired male and female singers, and a harem as well—the delights of a man's heart. I became greater by far than anyone in Jerusalem before me. In all this my wisdom stayed with me.*

In this insightful statement by King Solomon we see a man who experienced everything that life could offer a man and still he was seeking more! As wisdom stayed with him throughout this time he soon concludes it is all vanity, a chasing after the wind. The mighty Solomon was a un paralleled king of the ancient world so the wisdom he gives us today is very noteworthy .

Ecclesiastes 2:11

"Yet when I surveyed all that my hands had done and what I had toiled to achieve, everything was meaningless, a chasing after the wind; nothing was gained under the sun."
The famed Solomon learned a life lesson the hard way. After many years of extensive accomplishment in every aspect of life, he comes to the realization that all he has done is vanity.

Ecclesiastes 3:1-9

"There is a time for everything, and a season for every activity under the heavens: a time to be born and a time to die, a time to plant and a time to uproot, a time to kill and a time to heal, a time to tear down and a time to build, a time to weep and a time to laugh, a time to mourn and a time to dance, a time to scatter stones and a time to gather them, a time to embrace and a time to refrain from embracing, a time to search and a time to give up, a time to keep and a time to throw away, a time to tear and a time to mend, a time to be silent and a time to speak, a time to love and a time to hate, a time for war and a time for peace."

In this famous saying by Solomon we can learn a great deal of wisdom about the things of life.

Ecclesiastes 12:1

"Remember your Creator in the days of your youth, before the days of trouble come"

We should always seek our Creator in our youth and develop a relationship with Him, if we do this He will be with us throughout our days on the earth, and always help us in our time of need

Ecclesiastes 12:13

"Now all has been heard, here is the conclusion of the matter, Fear God and keep his commandments, for this is the whole duty of man."

At the end of Solomon's extraordinary life he comes to the conclusion we should honor God in all our ways, for if we build our life on anything else, it is built in vain.

**In this picture we see the famous story of the two mothers
and their contested infant before King Solomon.**

Song of Songs

§

Author and Date   King Solomon was the author of this book. He wrote many of these songs and sayings during his reign as King of Israel. The date of this writing was around 965 B.C.

Synopsis   The Song of Solomon is a romantic poem written to exhort the virtues of love between a husband and his wife. The song or poem is a presentation of love and marriage in the Divine order. A man and woman are to live and experience the joys of companionship in all ways in their time together, both spiritually and physically. The poetry specifically takes the form of a communication between a husband (the king) and his wife (the Shulamite women). This book is uniquely divided into the three phases of any marriage relationship; the first phase is the courtship, the second is the wedding, and the third one is the extended maturation of the relationship. Initially this writing begins before the meeting and courtship stage of the relationship. The future bride desires to be with her fiancée and spend time with him so they can develop their relationship into something deep and meaningful. In this song the king constantly praises the beauty and wisdom of the woman, giving her great confidence both emotionally and spiritually. As the two move to the wedding night, they make love and consecrate themselves to each other, however, as the relationship grows through time, troubles do come, the troubles that often come between husbands and wives. As the relationship matures these two lovers do experience difficulties, but as time goes by they reconcile and grow stronger in their relationship of love.

NOTABLE VERSES

Song of Solomon 2:7

"Do not arouse or awaken love until it so desires."

In this verse, we understand that we cannot force love, but should leave it alone until it is ready to be revealed.

Song of Solomon 5:1

"Eat, O friends, and drink; drink your fill, O lovers."

When people marry, they should enjoy passion and love, this will keep the marriage strong!

Song of Solomon 8:6-7

"Place me like a seal over your heart, like a seal on your arm; for love is as strong as death, its jealousy unyielding as the grave. It burns like blazing fire, like a mighty flame. Many waters cannot quench love; rivers cannot wash it away. If one were to give all the wealth of his house for love, it would be utterly condemned."

We understand the power of love, especially how romantic love has a lot of power over the individuals who experience it. Often it is an all-consuming emotion and desire.

Isaiah

§

Author and Date   The book of Isaiah was primarily written by the prophet Isaiah, other unknown writers were involved with it's composition. The name Isaiah means *"God is Salvation."* This book was probably written between 740 and 680 B.C.

Synopsis   The Jewish prophet Isaiah was called to minister to the kingdom of Judah during a difficult time in their history. Judah was being threatened by Assyria in the north and Egypt in the south, but was delivered from destruction by God's mercy. Isaiah preached against the many sins of the land, but told the people that if they turned back to the Lord, his mercy and blessing was their guarantee for a great future. In Isaiah, we begin to understand God's judgment and salvation is for all people. Also in Isaiah, God reveals to his people that He is a *'Holy God'* and that sin must be dealt with, both at the national level as well as the personal level. However, Isaiah tells us that God is also a God of mercy, grace, and compassion and only because of these traits he will not allow Israel and Judah to be destroyed. Prophetically, throughout the book of Isaiah inferences are made about the coming Messiah, which we *'New Testament'* believers know as Jesus Christ. As we continue to read Isaiah, everyone learns the Messiah will one day rule in justice, righteousness and peace, and that His kingdom will be for everyone. We also learn the Messiah will suffer, and through his suffering the sin of all mankind will be atoned for, and healing will be available to all those who accept him. All throughout this book we see Isaiah telling of Jesus Christ, who is accurately referred to as the *'King of Kings'* and *'Prince of Peace.'*

NOTABLE VERSES

Isaiah 7:14

"The Lord himself will give you a sign: The virgin will be with child and will give birth to a son, and he will be called Immanuel."

Here is the famous prophecy about the birth of Jesus the Christ, as it is used in the Gospel of Luke.

Isaiah 9:6

"For to us a child is born, to us a son is given, and the government will be on his shoulders. And he will be called Wonderful Counselor, Mighty God, Everlasting Father, and Prince of Peace."

In this verse, we see some enlightening and powerful names of the '*Messiah*,' the Lord Jesus Christ.

Isaiah 14:12-13

"How you have fallen from heaven, O morning star, son of the dawn! You have been cast down to the earth, you who once laid low the nations. You said in your heart, "I will ascend to heaven; I will raise my throne above the stars of God; I will sit enthroned on the mount of assembly, on the utmost heights of the sacred mountain."

We understand the downfall of Satan was his Pride before God. Interestingly, we see at one time Satan had a high place in heaven, next to God.

Isaiah 40:6

A voice says, "Cry out."And I said, "What shall I cry?"All people are like grass, and all their faithfulness is like the flowers of the field. The grass withers and the flowers fall because the breath of the LORD blows on it. Surely the people are grass. The grass withers and the flowers fall, but the Word of God endures forever.

In this great scripture reference, we learn a couple of things. First of all that men are like the grass of the fields that are here one day and then soon blown away! We also learn the everlasting revelation that God's Word remains forever. In the New Testament the great revelation to mankind is revealed to us in the person of Jesus Christ, who was the eternal 'Word' who became flesh and dwelt among us!

Isaiah 40:31

"Those who hope in the LORD will renew their strength. They will soar on wings like eagles;
they will run and not grow weary, they will walk and not be faint."

In this verse we can draw strength in the truth that if we trust in the Lord he will renew our strength and bring us out of any difficulty in life.

Isaiah 53:5-6
"But he was pierced for our transgressions, he was crushed for our iniquities; the punishment that brought us peace was upon him, and by his wounds we are healed. We all, like sheep, have gone astray, each of us has turned to his own way; and the LORD has laid on him the iniquity of all."
Here is a verse concerning the suffering of Christ at the crucifixion and the promises given to those who accept his sacrifice on the Cross.

Isaiah 57:15
"I live in a high and holy place, but also with him who is contrite and humble in spirit, to revive the spirit of the humble, and to revive the heart of the contrite ones."
God lives in two places, on His throne in heaven and within the hearts of the humble.

Isaiah 61:1-3
"The Spirit of the Lord is on me, because He has anointed me to preach good news to the poor. He has sent me to bind up the broken hearted, to proclaim the year of the Lord's favor and the vengeance of our God, to comfort all who mourn, and provide for those who grieve in Zion! To bestow on them a crown of beauty instead of ashes, the oil of gladness instead of mourning, and the garment of praise instead of despair"
In this great verse of Scripture, we see the ministry of Jesus Christ on earth. We can see it again in the gospel of Luke when Christ speaks in a synagogue before the Jewish people for the first time in his public ministry.

Jeremiah

§

Author and Date The author of the book of Jeremiah was the dynamic Jewish Prophet Jeremiah. The name Jeremiah means *"God has uplifted."* This book was written between 630 and 580 B.C.

Synopsis The book of Jeremiah is about a call of repentance to the land of Judah. It is a warning that if the people do not heed the preaching of Jeremiah, and turn back to the Lord God, judgment is coming! In Jeremiah we see that it might be too late for Judah because of the sin and false worship in the land but Jeremiah continues to preach anyway. The book tells us that after the death of King Josiah, who was the last faithful king to God, the nation of Judah had turned and abandoned the Lord God and his Laws. As Jeremiah preaches, he compares Judah to a prostitute, or an adulterer, who has left their marriage partner to love another. This is not a new analogy. The Old Testament prophets occasionally used this description when they spoke to God's people about their failings. In Jeremiah we learn that although the Lord always gives nations and people time to repent, time had come and the judgment of God was to begin. The people knew earlier in Judah's life as a nation, God did relent in sending destruction to the land, but He would not do it this time. Later in the book, Jeremiah writes about the mighty King Nebuchadnezzar of Babylon invading the land of Judah and making it subject to him. During this time in history, the Babylonian army destroyed both Judah and Jerusalem and made the inhabitant's servants and slaves to their empire.

NOTABLE VERSES

Jeremiah 1:5

"Before I formed you in the womb I knew you, before you were born I set you apart; I appointed you as a prophet to the nations."

God knows us, even in the womb of our mothers, and has a fabulous design for our lives. It is our mission in life to find out what it is.

Jeremiah 17:9

"The heart is deceitful above all things and beyond cure. Who can understand it?"

The inner self, "*our heart*," can be deceitful and irresponsible, this is why prayer and knowledge of God's Word is so beneficial to know.

Jeremiah 29:10-11

"This is what the LORD says: 'When seventy years are completed for Babylon, I will come to you and fulfill my gracious promise to bring you back to this place. For I know the plans I have for you,' declares the LORD, 'plans to prosper you and not to harm you, plans to give you hope and a future.'"

Here we see God has successful and prosperous plans for our lives, but it is up to us to be available to Him.

**The prophet Jeremiah warns the people of Israel against idolatry.
Jeremiah was one of the greatest prophets of the Old Testament.**

Lamentations

§

Author and Date   The author of the book of Lamentations was probably the prophet Jeremiah. The word *"Lament"* means *"a song, poem or writing expressing grief,"* and this is what the prophet Jeremiah was certainly doing in this book. The book was likely written between 586 and 575 B.C. during or soon after the destruction of Jerusalem.

Synopsis   In Lamentations, the writer tells us because of the idolatry and sin of Judah, God's judgment has come. So God allows the Babylonians to pillage, rape and destroy the city of Jerusalem and the magnificent Temple of Solomon. The prophet Jeremiah is known as the *"weeping prophet"* and experienced all these tragedies. In experiencing them, this book is overwhelmingly about sad tidings and *"Laments,"* so the title of the book is quite fitting! Also in this book, Jeremiah explains that God used the Babylonians under King Nebuchennazar to bring judgment on Jerusalem and the Jews. The main reason for this judgment was because of the idolatry and spiritual pride of his people! However, at one point in Lamentations the writer brings enormous hope and inspiration to the people, telling them if they repent and call to God with a new heart and mind, blessing will come to them!

Notable Verses
Lamentations 3:22-23
"Because of the LORD's great love we are not consumed, for his compassions never fail. They are new every morning; great is your faithfulness."
Here, we see the heart of God. Even though we sin and fall short of his will and righteousness, He is always there to bless and comfort if we come fully to Him. The compassion and mercy of God extends to everyone, at all times. If we sin and fall short

of something one day, we can get rise the next day and experience a new beginning, regardless of our situation in life. He is there for us, we need only to ask in prayer for His grace and help.

Lamentations 5:19-22
"You, O LORD, reign forever; your throne endures from generation to generation. Why do you always forget us? Why do you forsake us so long? Restore us to yourself, O LORD, that we may return; renew our days as of old unless you have utterly rejected us and are angry with us beyond measure."
This is a testimony of God and his power. God sits on his throne in heaven, ruling and reigning over the nations of men, always watching for the right time to bless those who look to Him. In our lives sometimes it seems like the things we desire take a long time to come to pass, but God is never slow, he is always right on time.

Ezekiel

∫

Author and Date   The writer of the book of Ezekiel was the Jewish prophet Ezekiel. The name Ezekiel means *"The Lord is Strong,"* this book was likely written between 593 and 565 B.C. during the Babylonian captivity of the Jews.

Synopsis   Ezekiel is about the life and ministry of the Jewish prophet Ezekiel, who lived during a difficult time in Israel's history. The theme of this book is primarily about the Lord God being acknowledged at all times, whether the times are good or bad!   Ezekiel, being a prophet, attempts to bring Israel to repentance, and then a new confidence in their future. Ezekiel taught; (1) God works through human messengers (2) Even in defeat and despair God's people need to affirm God's sovereignty, (3) God's Word never fails, (4) God is ever present and can be worshiped anywhere, (5) People must obey God if they expect to receive blessings, and lastly, God's Kingdom will come! In looking at Ezekiel's life, we see that he was uprooted from his homeland and carted off to Babylon at the age of twenty-five, and for five years he lived there in uncertainty, then around age thirty a majestic vision of the Lord's glory came to him in Babylon and it was then he received his illustrious calling. The main revelation this priest/prophet discovered at this time was God was not only the God of Israel, but the God of heaven and of the earth! While he was in Babylon, God gave Ezekiel a divine message for the people, even though the people were in bondage. The message he preached at this time gave them hope and assurance for a better tomorrow. When Ezekiel conveyed the messages God wanted to give to the people of Israel, he often delivered the messages in strange and unusual ways, but behind this unorthodox delivery there was always an exciting revelation.

NOTABLE VERSES

Ezekiel 2:3-6

"He said: 'Son of man, I am sending you to the Israelites, to a rebellious nation that has rebelled against me; they and their fathers have been in revolt against me to this very day. The people to whom I am sending you are obstinate and stubborn. Say to them, "This is what the Sovereign LORD says." And whether they listen or fail to listen - for they are a rebellious house - they will know that a prophet has been among them.'"

Often the Lord would send his prophets to the people of Israel to tell them to straighten out their lives before God, sadly more often than not they would not listen, and judgment would come to them.

Ezekiel 18:4

"For every living soul belongs to me, the father as well as the son , both alike belong to me. And the soul who sins is the one who will die."

In this scripture we see a great truth, which is God owns everyone and everything and sees all that mankind does.

Ezekiel 28:12-14

"'You were the model of perfection, full of wisdom and perfect in beauty. You were in Eden, the garden of God; every precious stone adorned you: ruby, topaz and emerald, chrysolite, onyx and jasper, sapphire, turquoise and beryl. Your settings and mountings were made of gold; on the day you were created they were prepared. You were anointed as a guardian cherub, for so I ordained you. You were on the holy mount of God; you walked among the fiery stones."

Here, we see a truth about Satan and his once lofty position in heaven, however we must remember that Satan is a fallen angel with limited power.

Ezekiel 33:11

"Say to them, 'As surely as I live, declares the Sovereign LORD, I take no pleasure in the death of the wicked, but rather that they turn from their ways and live. Turn! Turn from your evil ways! Why will you die, O house of Israel?'"

God never delights in the destruction of evil people but hopes all will come to Him and live.

Daniel

§

Author and Date   The writer of the book of Daniel was the prophet Daniel, the name Daniel means *"God is my judge."* This book may have been written around 530 B.C.

Synopsis   The book of Daniel is about the Babylonians conquering the kingdom of Judah around 605 B.C. In this war they brought many Jews into captivity to Babylon. Daniel was one of the most notable Israelites of this exile, because of this Daniel was placed in the court of Nebuchadnezzar, the King of Babylon. At this time he wrote down many of the experiences of his life in captivity. At the beginning of the writings of Daniel we learn about the fall of Jerusalem and the exile of the Jews to Babylonia. Although Daniel and some of his compatriots were placed in the palace of the King of Babylonia at this time, they were still essentially slaves. Due to his writings, we learn Daniel had many spiritual gifts, one gift was the ability to interpret dreams and because of this gift from God great promotion came to Daniel and his Hebrew friends Shadrach, Meschach and Abednego . Although Daniel and his Hebrew friends had become notable assistants to the King, there was mistrust and jealousy by some in the King of Babylon's court, because of this, Daniel and the three Hebrew young men were threatened but delivered miraculously by the hand of God. During Daniels tenure in court, he received several dreams and visions from God about the future of Israel, and also the world! In conclusion, the primary teaching found in the book of Daniel is about the Lord's sovereignty over the nations of men, and his judgments against mankind. However, we also learn about the Lord's faithfulness to those who honor Him.

Notable Verses

Daniel 2:31

"You looked, O king, and there before you stood a large statue - an enormous, dazzling statue, awesome in appearance."

In one of Daniel's dreams, he saw the *'King of Babylon'* as the undisputed leader of this region of the world at this time. This time in history has great historical significance to us today.

Daniel 3:17-18

"If we are thrown into the blazing furnace, the God we serve is able to save us from it, and he will rescue us from your hand, O king. But even if he does not, we want you to know, O king that we will not serve your gods or worship the image of gold you have set up."

Daniel's faith was tested by Nebuchadnezzar, even to the point of death, but as Daniel was faithful to God, the Lord was faithful to him and saved from this dramatic trial.

Daniel 4:34-35

"His dominion is an eternal dominion; his kingdom endures from generation to generation. All the peoples of the earth are regarded as nothing. He does as he pleases with the powers of heaven and the peoples of the earth. No one can hold back his hand or say to him: 'What have you done'"

In the verse we learn God Almighty and his kingdom is sovereign over everything. When we study the Bible, one of the all-consuming themes is the Lord God is the highest authority in the universe. Interestingly, in the Hebrew language we learn about a wonderful phrase about one of his names of His greatness. He is called *'El Elyon'* which means the *'Most High God.'* In this definition of Him we can be assured that there is none like him or ever will be. Amen!

**In this painting we see the story of Daniel in the lion's
den calling upon God for his deliverance**

The books of the *"Minor Prophets"* of the Bible begin at this point in the Scriptures, there are twelve of them. They are the books of Hosea, Amos, Obadiah, Jonah, Micah, Nahum, Malachi, Joel, Habakkuk, Haggai, Zephaniah and Zechariah.

Hosea

§

Author and Date The author of the book of Hosea was the Jewish prophet Hosea, the name Hosea means "*Salvation*." The book was likely written around 725 B.C.

Synopsis   Hosea wrote this book to tell the Israelites that their God is a loving God and is faithful to bless his people when they remain faithful to Him. In Hosea, we see the analogy of God's love depicted as the long-suffering husband who still loves his unfaithful wife. Hosea's life is on display for us, for Hosea is married to a woman named Gomer, and she was unfaithful to him, but instead of leaving her, Hosea is called by God to return to her. Because of this story we see the inspiring analogy of God's love for idolatrous Israel, regardless of their sins. As Hosea describes his adulterous wife, he relates to us the unfaithfulness of Israel to God by worshiping false deities. In Hosea, we learn that God does condemn and destroy, but does restore the people wholeheartedly, when they repent. Another powerful truth emphasized in the book of Hosea is God's love for his people and mankind altogether. For although multitudes have always gone their own way in their lives since the creation of man on the earth God has always been gracious and compassionate to everyone, whether they turn to Him or not. Towards the end of Hosea, we see the restoration of Israel and the great blessing given to them for returning to the Lord.

Notable Verses
Hosea 2:23
"I will plant her for myself in the land; I will show my love to the one I called 'Not my loved one.' I will say to those called 'Not my people,' 'You are my people'; and they will say, 'You are my God.'"

In this verse we see a promise to the Gentiles that through Jesus Christ they too will be called God's people.

Hosea 6:6
"For I desire mercy, not sacrifice, and acknowledgment of God rather than burnt offerings."
In this great scripture, we see the desire of the Lord God. We learn He values loving actions and praise from us, not religious rituals.

Hosea 14:2-4
"Take words with you and return to the LORD. Say to him: 'Forgive all our sins and receive us graciously, that we may offer the fruit of our lips. Assyria cannot save us; we will not mount war-horses. We will never again say "Our gods" to what our own hands have made, for in you the fatherless find compassion.' "I will heal their waywardness and love them freely, for my anger has turned away from them.'"
Here, we understand God's compassion and kindness to the repentant, not judgment! All throughout the ancient times, The Lord longed to be gracious and compassionate to Israel his people, but they often turned from Him, but the Lord always forgave them and blessed them.

Joel

§

Author and Date   The author of the book of Joel was the Jewish prophet Joel, interestingly, the name Joel means *"The Lord is God."* This book may have been written sometime between 835 and 800 B.C.

Synopsis   The nation of Judah is where this writing takes place during a time when a plague of locusts had devastated the land. This plague wipes out everything; the farms, the vineyards and all the agriculture in the area. The prophet Joel preaches to the people the locusts are like a foreign army and proclaims it is the judgment of the Lord against the land of Judah. However, in Joel's preaching he also proclaims that although this terrible event has taken place, God through his Spirit will bless the land again. Although Joel writes that the locusts and famine that have come is a Judgment from God, he emphasizes that a foreign army from one of the nations that surrounds Judah can bring even more trouble to them unless they repent and embrace the laws of the Lord their God.   Joel insists the people fast, pray and humble themselves as they seek God's forgiveness and blessing. He reminds them that if they do this, both spiritual and material blessing will come to them. Joel, in this book, also mentions the *"Day of the Lord"* and it's coming to all of mankind. This is something believers throughout the centuries have been reminded about in scriptures, for it is described as a frightful event, especially for those who have rejected the Lord God in their lives. The *"Day of the Lord"* is the most prominent revelation in this book, especially to the Christian believer, because we know much more about this event then those of ancient Israel. The basic theme of this *day* is the Lord reveals His power, glory and holiness to all.

Notable Verses

Joel 1:4

"What the locust swarm has left the great locusts have eaten; what the great locusts have left the young locusts have eaten; what the young locusts have left other locusts have eaten."

Here was a time when total judgment comes to Israel with nothing left but emptiness in the land of Israel. God's judgment can be devastating to both individual and a nation.

Joel 2:25

"I will repay you for the years the locusts have eaten."

Here, we understand that when God's judgment is over, either against a nation or a person, the Lord wants to bless and restore all that was lost during the trial and tribulation that occurred.

Joel 2:28

"And afterward, I will pour out my Spirit on all people. Your sons and daughters will prophesy, your old men will dream dreams, your young men will see visions."

In this scripture, we see the fulfillment of God's promise to give the *'Holy Spirit'* to all, which coincides with the beginning of the establishment of the Church after the resurrection of Christ!

Amos

§

Author and Date   The author of the book of Amos was the prophet Amos, who was from the city of Tekoa which is just south of Jerusalem, this book was likely written around 760 B.C.

Synopsis   Amos was a shepherd and farmer from a Judean village called Tekoa when God called him to minister to Israel. There was prosperity and peace in the land at this time, so his message of judgment and destruction for the nation went largely unheeded, especially by the leaders of the nation. The King at this time was a man named Jeroboam, and as Amos preached against the sins of idolatry, paganism, oppression and deceitfulness in high places his words fell on deaf ears. This was often the case when the people of Israel were enjoying immense prosperity. In the beginning of his ministry, Amos pronounces judgment against the pagan nations, then later upon Judah and Israel. In reading the book of Amos we are reminded that although God does judge his people, the Lord God is rich in mercy and promises blessing and restoration for the faithful.

Notable Verses
Amos 3:7
"Surely the Sovereign LORD does nothing without revealing His plan to His servants the prophets."
Here, we understand God often speaks through his anointed leaders! He always looks for someone he can trust and reveal himself to. Although He does not need any man or any help in accomplishing his will, he has given us the opportunity to rule and reign with Him forever through knowing his extraordinary purpose.

Amos 9:14

"I will bring back my exiled people Israel; they will rebuild the ruined cities and live in them. They will plant vineyards and drink their wine; they will make gardens and eat their fruit."

God always promises restoration to his people if they turn to Him. In this promise, the Lord brings Israel back to the Promised Land and blessed them abundantly.

Obadiah

§

Author and Date   The author of the book of Obadiah was the Jewish prophet Obadiah, the name Obadiah means *"Servant of the Lord."* This book was likely written around 840 B.C.

Synopsis   Obadiah is the shortest book in the Old Testament, however, it does give us some terrific wisdom on how God deals with the nations of the earth. The book is primarily about the Edomites, the descendants of Esau, who was the brother of the patriarch Jacob. We must remember that the descendants of Jacob were of the holy lineage, an unbroken line of people who were to live in the promises of God. Unfortunately, the descendants of Esau were not included in this lineage. There was a division between these two families for centuries, and in the writings of Obadiah we learn that there was an area of land that the children of Israel were not allowed to travel through on their exodus from Egypt, which was the land of the Edomites. At that time judgment from God was delayed against the Edomites, it was even delayed for many years, but now it was time for the Lord God to act in judgment against them. Obadiah is the prophet who now condemns Edom for this sin against both God and Israel. Obadiah's message to the people is that the kingdom of Edom will be utterly destroyed. Edom was arrogant, selfish and unwilling to help Israel when needed, and even worked to destroy the nation of Israel, so God's judgment comes to Edom.

NOTABLE VERSES
Obadiah 4
"Though you soar like the eagle and make your nest among the stars, from there I will bring you down," declares the LORD.

Here, we learn that often nations or people have high hopes of their lives and its success, but if the nation or person is not built upon the Lord God, the people build it in vain.

Obadiah 12
"You should not look down on your brother in the day of his misfortune, nor rejoice over the people of Judah in the day of their destruction, nor boast so much in the day of their trouble." We understand that we should never rejoice in other people's misfortune and painful times, God hates this.

Obadiah 15
"The day of the LORD is near for all nations. As you have done, it will be done to you; your deeds will return upon your own head."
In this verse, we can see the principle of the golden rule being the example we must always adhere to in life, for if we treat others well, good things will ultimately come our way.

Jonah

§

Author and Date   The author of the book of Jonah was the prophet Jonah, his name means "*Dove.*" This book was likely written between 793 and 758 B.C.

Synopsis   The book of Jonah is actually not about Jonah living in the belly of a whale for three days as many believe, it is about obeying the voice of the Lord, and God's extraordinary mercy. At the beginning of the book we learn Jonah is fearful and disobedient to the call of God in his life, which not only affects his own wellbeing but that of the people of Nineveh. As Jonah's anxiety and personal vanity cause him to flee from his assignment from God, which is to go to Nineveh and preach repentance to the people of this ancient city, Jonah wrongly believes that these people will be destroyed by God's judgment regardless of what he does. So in fear he runs away from his calling and boards a ship for Tarshish, which ironically is in the opposite direction of Nineveh. Once aboard the ship heading for Tarshish a massive storm ensues and all on board of the ship conclude that the runaway preacher Jonah is the cause. In ancient times, this was a normal belief, for when trouble came to a group of people they sometimes would cast lots to decide who was the cause of the problem. So in this case the crew of the ship cast lots and decided Jonah was the problem and threw him overboard. When this happened, Jonah was subsequently swallowed by a great fish, and while he was in the belly of this sea beast for 3 days, Jonah readily repented and said yes to the call of God in his life. After the three days were over, he was vomited up onto the land. The repentant Jonah then goes to Nineveh to fulfill his calling and begins to preach. As he preaches God's judgment to Nineveh, the people do something that Jonah did not think would happen, which was they repented of their sins and turned to the living God. Interestingly, instead of Jonah being joyful about this, he was dismayed over the repentance of the city and even confronts God about this remarkable situation. God then teaches Jonah a powerful lesson about mercy, and Jonah the preacher repents of his actions and worships God!

Notable Verses

Jonah 1:3
"But Jonah ran away from the LORD and headed for Tarshish."
How often this happens to many of us who are called by God, instead of receiving the call of God with joy and obedience, we run from the situation and in doing so make our lives harder than it has to be. If we embrace God's will for our lives there is perfect peace and joy.

Jonah 1:17
"But the LORD provided a great fish to swallow Jonah, and Jonah was inside the fish three days and three nights."
In this verse we see the famous whale story of Jonah, the real lesson here is when we run from God we usually end up in an uncomfortable place we do not want to be.

Jonah 2:2
"In my distress, I called to the LORD, and He answered me. From the depths of the grave I called for help, and you listened to my cry."
Whenever we find ourselves in a difficult position, we should pray to the Lord and ask for his help. For God is rich in mercy, and certainly can help us in any of our difficulties in life.

Jonah 3:10
"When God saw what they did and how they turned from their evil ways; He had compassion and did not bring upon them the destruction he had threatened."
In this verse, we see the mercy of God. He never wants to send judgment on a nation or an individual but always wants to send mercy, health and prosperity.

Jonah tries to flee from God's will, but he only experiences trouble

Micah

§

Author and Date   The author of the book of Micah was the Jewish prophet Micah, the word Micah means "*Who is like the Lord.*" This book was likely written between 735 and 686 B.C.

Synopsis   The prophet Micah was like a modern day civil rights leader, he strongly condemns the leaders, priests, and religious community of Israel for their hypocrisy and sin. It is because of these people, and their actions that Jerusalem will be destroyed, and the nation will go into exile! In this book the prophet proclaims a powerful message about the Lord's requirements for justice and right living, in doing this, he also tells of the judgment coming to the Israelites who have followed the teachings of false prophets and leaders. Micah's message to the people is one of judgment, and also hope. The prophecies of Micah primarily announce judgment upon Israel for its social evils, corrupt leadership and idolatry. Also in the book of Micah, there is a powerful prophecy concerning the coming of the Messiah from the tiny city of Bethlehem, this prophecy in Micah is often used around Christmas time by churches as a reminder of the humility of Christ coming to us. In this great passage of scripture, concerning Jesus Christ, we see him proclaimed as the righteous ruler of Israel.

NOTABLE VERSES
Micah 1:2
"Hear, O peoples, all of you, listen, O earth and all who are in it, that the Sovereign LORD may witness against you, the Lord from His holy temple."
In this verse we see the Lord God rendering His will and judgments upon the earth from His temple in heaven.

Micah 5:2

"But you, Bethlehem Ephrata, though you are small among the clans of Judah, out of you will come for me one who will be ruler over Israel, whose origins are from of old, from ancient times."

We have an outstanding prophecy concerning the coming of Jesus Christ in this scripture! For it was from the city of Bethlehem that the Savior of the world came to us, this scripture is often used on Christmas cards around the holidays.

Micah 6:8

"He has showed you, O man, what is good. And what does the LORD require of you? To act justly and to love mercy and to walk humbly with your God."

We understand in this scripture some of the basic things God wants from us, one of the most notable is to walk in humility before both God and man throughout our days.

Nahum

§

Author and Date   The author of the book of Nahum was an Israelite named Nahum. The name Nahum means *"Comfort."* We must always remember that our God is a God of *'comfort'* to all who call on Him. This book was written between 663 and 612 B.C.

Synopsis   The book of Nahum is about the impending judgment on the city of Nineveh. Years earlier God had sent Jonah to preach repentance to them, and the people listened and obeyed, therefore they did not receive punishment, however, in this case, it was too late! This generation refused to turn away from its sinful practices, so God's judgment was at hand. As mentioned, Nineveh once had responded to the preaching of Jonah and turned from their evil ways to serve the Lord God, but 150 years later, Nineveh returned to idolatry, violence and arrogance. So this time God sends Nahum to Nineveh preaching judgment and destruction to the city, but exhorting them to repentance so they can be blessed. Sadly, the Ninevites did not heed Nahum's warning, and the city was brought under the dominion of Babylon. The Assyrians, with their capitol city Nineveh, had become utterly brutal in their conquests (for example; doing things like hanging the bodies of their victims on poles and putting their skin on the walls of their tents). The Assyrians were Judah's avowed enemy, and many were afraid of them, so Nahum preached to the people of Judah to be strong and not to despair because God had pronounced judgment against the Assyrians.

NOTABLE VERSES
Nahum 1:7
"The LORD is good, a refuge in times of trouble. He cares for those who trust in him."

In this verse, we see that one of the great attributes about the Lord God is that He is good. He truly is! And if we look to Him and have faith in Him, all will be well in our lives. During our lives, it is reassuring to us that God is always there for us, whether it is in good times or bad times, He is always there.

Habakkuk

§

Author and Date   The author of the book of Habakkuk was the prophet Habakkuk, the name Habakkuk means something similar to *"grab"* or *"embrace,"* this book was likely written between 608 and 598 B.C.

Synopsis   In the book of Habakkuk we see this *'man of God'* questioning the Lord about certain things that are going on in the land, this is theme throughout this book. Habakkuk complains to God, and the Lord directly answers the prophet in often dramatic terms. The main question Habakkuk asks God is why He was allowing Israel to suffer at the hands of the surrounding nations, some of which were their mortal enemies. When Habakkuk prays to God for answers to this problem, the Lord replies to him about the unfaithfulness of Israel and their sins but promises good things in the future if they turn back to Him, which in turn restores the Habakkuk's faith.

Notable Verses
Habakkuk 1:2
"How long, Oh Lord, must I call for help, but you do not listen? Or cry out to you, 'Violence!' but you do not save."
In this verse we see a question that has always plagued God's people; why does the Lord not help us when we need Him? We have to understand that God's ways are not our ways, and He knows the beginning and end of all things, our job is to remain faithful to what we know, and to always acknowledge God in all things.

Habakkuk 1:5
"Look at the nations and watch and be utterly amazed. For I am going to do something in your days that you would not believe, even if I told you."
Here, the Lord God tells us he can do anything He wants to do, whenever He wants, with the only restriction being earlier promises he has made.

Habakkuk 3:19
"The Sovereign Lord is my strength; He makes my feet like the feet of a deer, He enables me to go on the heights."
God is our strength throughout life, and with Him we can do extraordinary things, if we turn our lives over to Him. When the Lord raise's us up to great heights in our life we must always remember Him when the blessings come, we should always give the glory to God.

Zephaniah

§

Author and Date   The author of the book of Zephaniah was the Jewish prophet Zephaniah. Interestingly, the name Zephaniah means *"Defended by God."* This book was likely written between 640 and 609 B.C. during the reign of King Josiah.

Synopsis   In the book of Zephaniah, like many of the other writings of the minor prophets, the message is abundantly clear to the people, which was the Lord God is sovereign over the nations and kingdoms of men and He is faithful to those who are good and godly, but to the wicked He will bring judgment upon them. In Zephaniah, God pronounces his judgments first to the world, then to Judah and Jerusalem, and then to the heathen nations. Zephaniah also proclaims the Lord's blessing will come to all nations and people if they come to Him in truth and honor. In the book of Zephaniah we are reminded that neither the false gods the people worship or the individual armies of nations can save them from God's judgment, for He is the Lord God of the universe. However, it is made clear in Zephaniah if they turn to the true and living God, He will be gracious and compassionate to everyone. Also, in Zephaniah we are reminded of a special day at the end of the time called the *"Day of the Lord,"* which is a day which will come to all mankind, when all the peoples of the earth will be judged for the lives they have lived.

Notable Verses
Zephaniah 1:18
"Neither their silver nor their gold will be able to save them on the day of the LORD's wrath. In the fire of his jealousy the whole world will be consumed, for he will make a sudden end of all who live in the earth."

Here, we see the arrogance and folly of many people concerning their lives, for when the Almighty God decides to judge, and even punish, there is absolutely nothing anyone can do.

Zephaniah 2:3
"Seek the LORD, all you humble of the land, you who do what he commands. Seek righteousness, seek humility; perhaps you will be sheltered on the day of the LORD's anger."
We understand in this scripture that if we seek the Lord in humility, all will go well with us, for our God is gracious and compassionate, slow to anger and abounding in love!

Zephaniah 3:17
"The LORD your God is with you, he is mighty to save. He will take great delight in you, he will quiet you with his love, he will rejoice over you with singing."
In this verse we learn that God delights in his people and even sings over us. What a glorious God we have!

Haggai

§

Author and Date   The author of the book Haggai was the Jewish prophet Haggai. The name Haggai means *"Festival"* or something like a religious party. This book was written around 520 B.C.

Synopsis   The book of Haggai is about putting God Almighty first place in our lives. At this time the people of Israel reversed their priorities and failed to put the Lord first place in their lives, so the nation of Judah was sent into Babylonian exile. When Judah was in this exile, God directed Cyrus the Persian king to allow the Jews in exile to go back to Jerusalem. In Haggai we learn of a group of Jews who returned to their land with great joy, and as they put God first place in their lives they started to rebuild the Temple in Jerusalem. However, they were met with opposition by the local people and Persian officials. Also at this time, the Lord wanted the re-building of the Temple to be the main priority of this group of people and not their own personal affairs. In this book, we see Haggai reminding the people not to be discouraged about the building itself because this Temple would not be as ornate as the first Temple, which was King Solomon's Temple. To motivate them to faith and hard work, Haggai also urges the people of Israel to turn from their sins and selfishness and trust in the Lord's power and authority, for if they do, God offers to bless the people for their obedience. Toward the end of Haggai, he emphasizes to the people the future promises they will receive will be splendid indeed.

NOTABLE VERSES
Haggai 1:4
"Is it a time for you yourselves to be living in your paneled houses, while this house remains a ruin?"

Here, we have in this verse of scripture a reminder to keep the things of God first place in our lives. In Old Testament times, the temple was God's house, but now we Christians are God's house, a living temple to the Lord.

Haggai 1:5-6
"Now this is what the LORD Almighty says: 'Give careful thought to your ways. You have planted much, but have harvested little. You eat, but never have enough. You drink, but never have your fill. You put on clothes, but are not warm. You earn wages, only to put them in a purse with holes in it.'"

Often in our lives we try to do the right things to get ahead, and we do all that we know how to do. But it seems we never get ahead, it seems like everything is in vain, but it is not in vain, for when we fail to achieve our goals, we can always go to God and ask for wisdom in our situations and He will give it to us, so we can go on and have success.

Haggai 2:9
"'The glory of this present house will be greater than the glory of the former house,' says the LORD Almighty. 'And in this place I will grant peace,' declares the LORD Almighty."

Sometimes in life we need to tear down the past to have a bright and better future!

Zechariah

Author and Date   The author of the book of Zechariah was the Jewish prophet Zechariah, interestingly the name Zechariah means *"the Lord remembers."* This book was likely written around 518 B.C.

Synopsis   In the book of Zechariah, the theme is about how God uses his prophets to teach and warn the people of Israel. Often, the people did not listen to them and refused to change their ways, therefore, God's judgment and punishment comes to them. Also in this book, we see that false prophets have arisen in the land and have become a constant problem. God warns the people that these men should be ignored, for at this time in Israel's history these false teachers were numerous. The book of Zechariah teaches us that salvation from the Lord is available to everyone, even to the Gentiles, for in the last chapter of this book we understand people from all over the world will ultimately worship the Lord, the Almighty God. The book of Zechariah reminds us that the Lord God is sovereign over this world, both the natural world and the spiritual world and that his ultimate will is going to be done, regardless of what anyone says or does.

NOTABLE VERSES
Zechariah 1:3
"Therefore tell the people: This is what the LORD Almighty says: 'Return to me,' declares the LORD Almighty, 'and I will return to you,' says the LORD Almighty."
In this verse, we understand that God is always ready and willing to have a relationship with us. All we have to do is call on the Lord through prayer and acknowledgement, and then look to Him for guidance in our lives.

Zechariah 9:9

"Rejoice greatly, O Daughter of Zion! Shout, Daughter of Jerusalem! See, your king comes to you, righteous and having salvation, gentle and riding on a donkey, on a colt, the foal of a donkey."

Here, we see a significant prophecy about Jesus Christ entering the city of Jerusalem, before the crucifixion and resurrection. There were multitudes of specific Old Testament prophecies fulfilled in the person of Jesus Christ, and this is one of them. Notice here in this verse how 'God the Son' comes to Jerusalem in the humility of riding a young donkey, this is a representation on how God comes to us, even today. He often deals with mankind with consummate gentleness and respect. This is something we all should rejoice in, for the creator of heaven and earth could deal with us quite differently.

Malachi

§

Author and Date The author of the book of Malachi was probably the Jewish prophet Malachi. The name Malachi means *"Messenger,"* and as we learn in this book Malachi was certainly an ardent messenger for the Lord. This book was likely written around 475 B.C.

Synopsis The book of Malachi is the final book of the Old Testament, it was written about 400 years before the birth of Christ. The book tells us about *"The Word of the Lord"* coming to Israel through the prophet Malachi. The *"Word"* or message brought to Israel at this time was a warning to turn back to the Lord God. The people of Israel needed to understand that *faith* and God's *justice* must be done in the land, or trouble was on the horizon. At this time the temple had been rebuilt in Jerusalem but there was little blessing in the land. The reason for this according to the prophet was because the people of God had gone astray, especially the leaders and priests. The main reason for this was the priests and the people were not being honest in the offerings and sacrifices to God, for many were using blemished animals for their offerings and sacrifices, which were in direct violation of the *Law of Moses*, and others were withholding the *tithe* and using it for their own selfish desires. The personal conduct of the Israelites was abhorrent for a people who were called to live good and holy lives before God and man. Although these people had turned away from the laws of God, the Lord promised to be good to them if they would embrace His ways again. At the end of this book we see a significant prophecy concerning the coming of John the Baptist, the forerunner of Jesus Christ.

NOTABLE VERSES
Malachi 1:6
"A son honors his father and a servant his master. If I am a father, where is the honor due me? If I am a master, where is the respect due me? Says the Lord Almighty. It is you, O priests, who show contempt for my name."

Here we see the Lord telling his people that He, the Lord God of the universe, should be first place in their lives, that He must be honored above all. The way we can show him his due honor is to be faithful in everything we do in our lives, even if it seems small and insignificant.

Malachi 3:6-7
"I the Lord do not change. So you, O descendants of Jacob are not destroyed. Ever since the time of your forefathers you have turned away from my decrees and have not kept them. Return to me, and I will return to you, says the Lord Almighty."

In this verse, we understand that God Almighty is eternal and unchanging. People change and the things of life change, but our God does not. He is the same yesterday, today and forever. We can take considerable comfort in this great revelation.

The New Testament

§

In this famous picture, the four Gospel writers are seen receiving inspiration from the Holy Spirit. Many scholars believe Mark's Gospel was the first New Testament book written. The four Gospels are the central books of the New Testament. They point to God's revelation to mankind in the person of Jesus Christ.

The Gospel of Matthew

§

Author and Date   The author of the Gospel of Matthew was written by one of the original 12 apostles named Matthew. The name Matthew means "*Gift from God.*" This apostle was a tax collector when he was called by the Lord to follow Him. He probably wrote this gospel in the city of Antioch around 55 to 60 A.D. At this time most Christians were Jewish converts, so he emphasized a Jewish perspective in this gospel.

Synopsis   In the book of Matthew the writer intends to proclaim to the Jews, and then to the Gentiles that Jesus Christ is the promised Messiah. This is the all-encompassing message of this Gospel. In the Gospel of Matthew there are often quotes from the Old Testament to show how Jesus fulfilled the prophecies of the ancient Jewish prophets. In the first few chapters of Matthew he tells us of the lineage, birth, and early life of Christ, and then goes on from there into the ministry of Jesus. Interestingly, in reading about the ministry of Jesus Christ, we see that many of Christ's teachings are actual sermons, like the famous '*Sermon on the Mount.*' We also see parables and storytelling as a main teaching method used by the Lord throughout this Gospel. In the last several chapters of the book, we learn about the arrest, trial, and crucifixion of Jesus Christ. These incidents are written with exceptional accuracy as Matthew was an eyewitness to many of these historic events. At the very end of this Gospel we see the resurrection story and the command by our Lord for the '*Great Commission.*'

Notable Verses

Matthew 5:17

"Do not think that I have come to abolish the Law or the Prophets; I have not come to abolish them but to fulfill them."

In this statement by the Lord, we understand that one of the reasons Christ came into the world was to fulfill the ancient writings of the prophets long ago. The Christian church is built upon the Old Testament as well as the New Testament.

Matthew 5:43-44

"You have heard that it was said, 'Love your neighbor and hate your enemy.' But I tell you: Love your enemies and pray for those who persecute you."

Here, we see *'Love'* as the primary attribute for God's people. This teaching was revolutionary at the time the Lord spoke of it, for He told us not only to pray for people, but love them as well.

Matthew 6:9-13

"This is how you should pray: 'Our Father in heaven, hallowed be your name, your kingdom come, your will be done on earth as it is in heaven. Give us today our daily bread. Forgive us our debts, as we also have forgiven our debtors. And lead us not into temptation, but deliver us from the evil one. For yours is the kingdom, and the power, and the glory, forever. Amen"

Here, we have the *"Lord's Prayer."* In this famous prayer we see that praise to God is given at the beginning of it, this is how all our prayers should begin. After this, we learn that God wants heaven's will to be done here on earth. In heaven there is righteousness, peace and joy, all of the time. We also learn asking God for our daily needs is something we should do, not just for daily necessities, but for all our needs. At the end of this prayer, we learn God never tempts us with evil as some think, but always gives us deliverance from evil if we seek Him in our daily lives.

Christ teaching in a synagogue

Matthew 16:26
"What good will it be for a man if he gains the whole world, yet loses his soul? Or what can a man give in exchange for his soul?"
In this scripture we understand in the sight of God one human being is worth all the riches, wealth and pleasures of this life.

Matthew 22:37-4
"You shall love the Lord your God with all your heart and with all your soul and with all your mind." This is the first and greatest commandment. And the second is: "Love your neighbor as yourself." All the Law and the Prophets hang on these two."
This is the greatest command to all of us! And honestly it is easy, for once you get to know the Lord God you can't help but love Him, and when the love of God dwells in you, being kind to your neighbor comes naturally.

Matthew 27:31
"After they had mocked him, they took off the robe and put his own clothes on him. Then they led him away to crucify him."
When *Jesus the Christ* was crucified, it was a horrific event. Roman crucifixion was an extremely painful punishment; however, to fulfill Old Testament prophecies Jesus went through this for all of mankind.

Matthew 28:5-6
"The angel said to the women, 'do not be afraid, for I know that you are looking for Jesus, who was crucified. He is not here; he has risen, just as he said. Come and see the place where he lay.'"
The three greatest words ever said in the last 2000 thousand years were; *"He is Risen"*! When Christ rose from that tomb He set in motion the Christian faith that would bring God and man together again.

Matthew 28:19-20
"Therefore go and make disciples of all nations, baptizing them in the name of the Father and of the Son and of the Holy Spirit, and teaching them to obey everything I have commanded you. And surely I am with you always, to the very end of the age."

Here, we see the Lord's impressive command to all believers. First we see baptism and its importance for all believers, and instruction that one should be baptized in the name of the Triune God. After this, we understand obeying the teachings from the Bible is a prerequisite for believers in their walk with God. At the end of this great statement we know that the Lord is always with us. This statement by God is extremely comforting to any believer.

The Gospel of Mark

§

Author and Date   The Gospel of Mark was written by a disciple named Mark, interestingly his name is taken from the Roman god "*Mars*." Mark was more than likely the John Mark in other New Testament writings, who was the same man who joined Paul and Barnabas on their first missionary journey. Many people believe the Gospel of Mark was one of the first books written in the New Testament, probably in the city of Rome around 55A.D.

Synopsis   Mark's gospel is targeted to '*Gentile*' or non-Jewish believers. Mark wrote as a leader in the early church to Christians who previously heard and believed the Gospel. It is apparent Mark wanted to give them a memoir account of Jesus Christ as a servant and savior of the world in order to strengthen their '*Faith*' in the face of severe persecution. Mark's Gospel is a basic account of Jesus Christ. It is simply written, swiftly going from one occurrence to another. It begins with the baptism of Jesus by his cousin *John the Baptist*, and from there goes into the beginning of Christ's earthly ministry. Later in the gospel we see Christ gaining disciples and ministering throughout Galilee and Judea. As the Lord begins to touch the lives of many people and strengthen his chosen followers, some of the Jews are not fully convinced that He is the '*Messiah*,' the '*Anointed one of Israel*,' which begins to cause conflict. As this gospel continues, Mark writes about the "*Passion week*," which is the last week of the life of Christ on earth. It is here we learn many details about Jesus, who He was, and what his mission was all about. In Mark's Passover week account we read about the trial, crucifixion, burial and resurrection of Jesus Christ, which in turn fulfills all of Old Testament scriptures.

NOTABLE VERSES

Mark 1:11

"And a voice came from heaven: 'You are my Son, whom I love; with you I am well pleased.'"

Here, we see God the Father giving us acknowledgement of who Jesus Christ was. We must always remember the Father and Son are one, as we continue to see throughout scripture. Interestingly when we become a child of God we learn that the same love the Father has for the Son is the same love he has for us!

Mark 1:17

"'Come, follow me,' Jesus said, 'and I will make you fishers of men.'"

When Jesus calls someone to follow Him, the purpose is always twofold; it is to serve both God and man. Christ always comes to us as we are and often uses our background to accomplish God's great purpose in our lives.

John the Baptist preaches to Israel around 30 A.D.

Mark 10:45
"For even the Son of Man did not come to be served, but to serve, and to give His life as a ransom for many."
Service is always what God calls us to do, and there can be no better example of this than Christ, as He being *'God incarnate'* became a servant to all.

Mark 12:33
"'Love the Lord your God will all your heart and with all your soul and with all your mind and with all your strength.' The second is this: 'Love your neighbor as yourself.'"
Here, we have the greatest commandment in all of scripture. Which is to love the Lord God fully, but to do this we must know him in a relationship like a child and a father. To love our fellow man fully we must always be available to meet their needs.

Mark 16:6
"Don't be alarmed, he said. 'You are looking for Jesus the Nazarene, who was crucified. He has risen! He is not here. See the place where they laid Him."
When the angel spoke these words to Mary, he opened up a new world for mankind forever! In the resurrection Jesus fulfilled the Old Testament prophecies about his life.

Mark 16:15
"He said to them, 'Go into all the world and preach the good news to all creation.'"
In this command from the Lord, we understand that all believers have a role in proclaiming the *'Good News'* that Jesus Christ is Lord over everything.

The Gospel of Luke

§

Author and Date   The author of the Gospel of Luke was the gentile physician Luke, who was a close companion of the apostle Paul. Interestingly, Luke was the only gentile (non-Jew) to write any of the New Testament books. Luke's name means *"one from the area of Luciana"* which was a region of Italy in ancient times. The Gospel of Luke was probably written between 58 and 65A.D.

Synopsis   The Gospel of Luke is often called the most beautiful book ever written. Luke begins by telling us about Joseph and Mary, the birth of John the Baptist, and the journey of Mary and Joseph to Bethlehem, where Christ was born. After this, Luke begins to emphasize the compassion of Jesus Christ, which is reflected throughout this Gospel by dynamic preaching and storytelling. Luke relates to the reader that while many believe in Christ's love and compassion, others, especially the religious leaders, challenge and oppose the ministry and claims of Jesus Christ. Toward the end of this Gospel, Jesus is betrayed, tried and crucified, and then the glorious resurrection occurs, which fulfills all biblical prophecy.

Notable Verses
Luke 1:1-4
Many have undertaken to write an account of the things that have been fulfilled among us, just as they were handed down to us by those who from the first were eyewitnesses and servants of the word. With this in mind, since I myself have carefully investigated everything from the beginning, I too decided to write an orderly account for you, most excellent Theophilus, so that you may know the certainty of the things you have been taught.

In this Gospel writing we learn Luke was not an eyewitness to the life of Christ but attained a multitude of evidence to write about this account of Jesus Christ. Everything written in this account was thoroughly investigated by Luke, which is corroborated by the other Gospels.

Luke 2:4-7

"So Joseph also went up from the town of Nazareth in Galilee to Judea, to Bethlehem the town of David, because he belonged to the house and line of David. He went there to register with Mary, who was pledged to be married to him and was expecting a child. While they were there, the time came for the baby to be born, and she gave birth to her firstborn, a son. She wrapped him in swaddling clothes and placed him in a manger because there was no room for them in the inn."

During this time in history, Israel was under the control of Rome, and there was a Census placed on the land with which Joseph and Mary had to comply. This part of the story reminds us how awesome God's timing is in our lives, because for Scripture to be fulfilled about Christ, he had to be born in Bethlehem at a certain time, and only a census by a pagan ruler could bring it about.

Luke 4:18-19, 21

"'The Spirit of the Lord is on me, because he has anointed me to preach good news to the poor. He has sent me to proclaim freedom for the captives and recovery of sight for the blind, to release the oppressed, to proclaim the year of the Lord's favor.' Today this scripture is fulfilled in your hearing."

In this scripture reference, Jesus was using a verse in the Old Testament from the book of Isaiah to prove once again his *'Messiahship'*! Notice in this scripture what the attributes of the Messiah would be. He would not only preach, but heal all and bring God's favor to everyone who accepted it.

Luke 6:27

"Love your enemies, do good to those who hate you, bless those who curse you, pray for those who mistreat you."

Here, we see a landmark teaching by Jesus Christ, He was telling believers to do the opposite of what natural instinct says to do in certain circumstances. The blessing in obeying the Lord in this way is God Himself will come into the situation and give skillful deliverance.

The Nativity scene

Luke 6:37
"Do not judge and you will not be judged."
In this powerful verse there is a universal law that takes place, the law that relates to us is this; the measure of mercy you show towards someone when they do something wrong, will be the same measure you receive, when you do wrong.

Luke 12:6

"Are not five sparrows sold for two pennies? Yet not one of them is forgotten by God. Indeed, the very hairs of your head are all numbered."

Here, we see how much our Creator thinks about us as individuals. He knows more about us than we do. This is why we should trust Him fully.

Luke 18:31-32

"Jesus took the twelve aside and told them, 'We are going up to Jerusalem, and everything that is written by the prophets about the Son of Man will be fulfilled. He will be handed over to the Gentiles. They will mock him, insult him, spit on him, flog him and kill him, and on the third day He will rise again.'"

In this verse, Jesus is telling us of the Old Testament prophecies that had to be fulfilled in order for Him to be mankind's Savior. He fulfilled every single one of them! We must always remember that Roman crucifixion was a very painful and bloody affair, but Christ endured its shame for us. In enduring the crucifixion, Christ not only took upon himself the sins of the world, but also every disease and sickness known to mankind. The apostle Peter writes of this great revelation when he tells us in his letter 1st Peter.

The Last Supper

Luke 23:33-34

"When they came to the place called the Skull, there they crucified him, along with the criminals—one on his right, the other on his left. Jesus said, 'Father, forgive them, for they know not what they are doing.'"

This scripture gives us insight into the crucifixion of the Lord. Jesus went to the cross for our sakes, even though he did not want to. We learn Christ was even merciful on the Cross, especially to those who crucified Him. This shows us the nature of our God, for even when people reject Him, he offers mercy and love.

Luke 24:1-7

"On the first day of the week, very early in the morning, the women took the spices they had prepared and went to the tomb. They found the stone rolled away from the tomb, but when they entered, they did not find the body of the Lord Jesus." In their fright the women bowed down with their faces to the ground, but the men said to them, "Why do you look for the living among the dead? He is not here; he has risen! Remember how he told you, while he was still with you in Galilee: 'The Son of Man must be delivered over to the hands of sinners, be crucified and on the third day be raised again.' "

Here we have '*Easter Sunday*,' and the story of the disciple Mary when she first heard the greatest statement ever; "*He is risen*." When Christ rose from the dead he liberated mankind from their sins and fears forever, and brought all who would receive him eternal life! The interesting thing about the resurrection of Jesus and the empty tomb is that it was the women disciples who were the first people on the scene to hear the message of the living Christ spoken from the angels.

*Luke 24:44-4*7

" He said to them, This is what I told you while I was still with you: Everything must be fulfilled that is written about me in the Law of Moses, the Prophets and the Psalms. Then he opened their minds so they could understand the Scriptures. He told them, This is what is written: The Messiah will suffer and rise from the dead on the third day, and repentance for the forgiveness of sins will be preached in his name to all nations, beginning at Jerusalem."

Jesus Christ fulfilled all the Old Testament requirement for Him to be the Messiah! This is why it is important for all Christians to have quality knowledge of the Old Testament just like the first apostles had. This is very important for those who want to grow in the knowledge and grace of God.

Angels were at the empty tomb after the resurrection of Christ

The Gospel of John

§

Author and Date   The apostle John was the author of this Gospel. He was one of the closest apostles to the Lord, and an eyewitness to the life of Christ. Interestingly, John's name means "*the Lord is gracious.*" The book was probably written in the city of Ephesus around 90 A.D.

Synopsis   The main emphasis in the Gospel of John is that everyone who reads it would believe in Jesus Christ and experience life in Him. While the other Gospels emphasized the full life story of Christ, John emphasizes; "*Jesus Christ as God incarnate.*" The timeframe of the Gospel of John is actually only three years of Christ's ministry on earth. The major theme of this book always reminds the reader that Jesus Christ was '*God the Son,*' who is both fully God and fully man! Another important theme of John's gospel is that it's a theological text using a lot of the Old Testament as its background. In the beginning of the book John's gospel introduces the reader to Christ, not from his birth, but from '*the beginning*' as the '*Word,*' who as *Deity.* Who was involved in every aspect of creation, and who later becomes flesh in order that He may take away the world's sin. In the theology of Christ being Divine, John wanted everyone to understand that Jesus Christ was God's great sacrifice for God Himself. Throughout the gospel, John always emphasizes Jesus as the Messiah and through him there is salvation for all who accept him. Toward the end of John's gospel we see Christ exhorting his disciples to remain faithful to what they have been taught, and to look for the glorious appearing of the Holy Spirit. At the end of the Gospel we read in dramatic detail the story of the trial, death by crucifixion and the resurrection of Jesus Christ with his final proclamations to believers.

Notable Verses

John 1:1-4

"In the beginning was the Word, and the Word was with God, and the Word was God. And the Word became flesh and dwelt among us, and we beheld His glory, the glory as of the only begotten of the Father, full of grace and truth."

In this verse, we see one of the most powerful verses of scripture in the Bible. The finite mind cannot sometimes fully comprehend some of the great truths of the Bible, but here we understand the nature of God. The pre- incarnate '*Word*' comes to us as '*God*' himself, for they are one, so in Jesus Christ we have God clothed in flesh, both fully God and fully man!

John 1:29

"The next day John saw Jesus coming toward him, and said, 'Behold! The Lamb of God who takes away the sin of the world!'"

In Jesus Christ we have God's sacrifice for the sins of mankind, nothing else would satisfy the Creator but the true holiness found in the Son of God! We also learn here the Son of God was the fruition of all the Old Testament sacrifices necessary to bring people close to a Holy God. In Old Testament times the people had to do many rituals and sacrifices to approach God, but in Christ and our acceptance of him we have full right standing with Him.

John encounters Christ on the shore of Galilee, where he was a fisherman

John 3:16
"For God so loved the world that He gave His only begotten Son that whoever believes in Him should not perish but have everlasting life"
In this famous verse we understand that God loves mankind with an everlasting love, and provided for him a way to come into relationship with Him, which is through Jesus Christ.

John 10:10
"The thief comes to steal, to kill, and to destroy. I have come that they may have life and that they may have it more abundantly."
The thief here is Satan and his ways. We learn he wants more than anything else to destroy God's people, but Christ came to build us up and give us a life beyond measure.

Christ's first miracle was changing water into wine!

John 11:25-26
"Jesus said to her, 'I am the resurrection and the life. He who believes in me, though he may die, he shall live. And whoever lives and believes in me shall never die. Do you believe this?"

Here we see Jesus Christ giving us eternal life; we gain this by simply believing in Him!

John 13:35
"By this all will know that you are my disciples, if you love one another"

Here we understand the immense virtue of love, this type of love is the pre-eminent quality that the Christian should have in his or her life.

John 14:6
"Jesus said to him, 'I am the way, the truth, and the life. No one comes to the Father except through me"

In this great verse of Scripture we understand that Jesus Christ proclaimed who he was, and how he was mankind's gateway to the God of heaven and earth.

John 14:9
"Jesus said to him, 'Have I not been with you so long, and yet you have not known Me, Philip? He who has seen me has seen the Father; so how can you say, "Show us the Father"?' "I and the Father are one"!

Here, once again Jesus tells us who He was; we can understand that Jesus Christ was God incarnate. In this scripture is also a further explanation of the Trinity, for we can see that *'The Father, The Son, and The Holy Spirit'* are equal and separate, but still one! It is sometimes hard for our finite minds to comprehend such things as the *'Trinity,'* but still we must take it by faith and believe.

In this picture we see Pontius Pilate giving the people a choice of either freeing Jesus the Christ or Barabbas

John 20:29
"Jesus said to him, 'Thomas, because you have seen me, you have believed. Blessed are those who have not seen and yet believe'"
In this verse, we can understand the kind of *'Faith'* that God wants from us, for us to believe without seeing is something remarkable in the sight of the Lord. *Faith* is a gift that must be received, then opened and exercised, to be of any value.

The crucifixion scene of Jesus Christ

Acts

§

Author and Date   The author of Acts was Luke the physician, who was a companion of the apostle Paul. The word Acts means *"anything or something being done,"* and in this case it is about the *"Acts"* of the early church. The book of Acts was likely written sometime between 61-64 A.D. Many Christians believe it is a continuation of the Gospel of Luke.

Synopsis   The book of Acts gives us a bird's eye view of the early church. The *'Holy Spirit,'* the third person of the *'Trinity'* is the foundation of this writing. The witness and power of the *'Spirit of God'* is the dominant reality throughout this book. The *'Acts'* of the first believers are recorded from the beginning days of the church in Jerusalem to the outer reaches of the Roman Empire. The Holy Spirit was promised to the Church by Jesus Christ himself, and once the first believers received this gift from the Lord they quickly learned of the many endowments and power given to them. The new believers also realized that when the *'Holy Spirit'* and the *'Word of God'* were proclaimed together, many miracles did abound, which gave the Church added power in establishing itself in a dark world at this crucial time. The book of Acts is also a history book of the time, for not only did the new Christian church spread the gospel of Jesus Christ around the world, but influential individuals, communities and even nations were impacted by the gospel message. Saul of Tarsus, who later became the apostle Paul, was once a Jewish Pharisee and persecutor of the Church is the most influential person in this book. As Paul preached the Gospel in the power of the Holy Spirit, and ministered throughout the Roman world, the church grew significantly. The book of Acts ends with Paul's imprisonment in Rome and the Kingdom of God being proclaimed to all.

NOTABLE VERSES

Acts 1:8

"But you will receive power when the Holy Spirit comes on you, and you will be my witnesses in Jerusalem, and in all Judea and Samaria, and to the ends of the earth."

Here, we have a powerful statement of what the new Church was all about, for when the *'Holy Spirit'* came upon believers after the resurrection of Jesus Christ, the *'Spirit of God'* entered the earth in a bold and dynamic way. This gave the early Christians the power to establish the Church in the tumultuous 1st century. The command to go into the entire world and proclaim the *'Good News'* about Jesus Christ was given to these believers, and history tells us that they turned a dark and evil world into a world filled with the light, and the love of God.

Acts 2:4

"All of them were filled with the Holy Spirit and began to speak in other tongues as the Spirit enabled them."

In this verse, we see one of the gifts of the Holy Spirit being mentioned. The gift of tongues is the least of all spiritual gifts but it does give believers immense inspiration and strength when praying.

The Holy Spirit descends on believers in Jerusalem on the day of Pentecost, some fifty days after the resurrection of Jesus Christ which we know as Easter Sunday. Many believers call this day the actual beginning of the Christian church

Acts 4:12
"Salvation is found in no one else, for there is no other name under heaven given to men by which all are saved."

Here is a marvelous truth about the Lord. He was given to mankind so that all may be saved through Him.

Acts 4:19-20
"But Peter and John replied, 'Judge for yourselves whether it is right in God's sight to obey you rather than God. For we cannot help speaking about what we have seen and heard.'"
When the apostles Peter and John were filled with the Holy Spirit, they received extensive courage and strength to proclaim the good news about Jesus the Christ.

Peter and John minister to a lame man. Healing miracles were an earmark of the first Christians.

Acts 9:3-6

"As Saul neared Damascus on his journey, suddenly a light from heaven flashed around him. He fell to the ground and heard a voice say to him, 'Saul, Saul, why do you persecute me?' 'Who are you, Lord?' Saul asked. 'I am Jesus, whom you are persecuting,' he replied. 'Now get up and go into the city, and you will be told what you must do.'"

In this verse the dramatic conversion experience of the apostle Paul occurs. Notice in this statement by the Lord that when he was speaking to Paul he said *"why do you persecute me?"* This tells us it is not only we as individuals who are persecuted when someone stands against us, but it is the *'Lord God'* himself. Later on, as we know, Paul becomes one of the greatest Christians who ever lived and wrote many of the letters of the New Testament.

Acts 16:31

"So they said, 'Believe on the Lord Jesus Christ, and you will be saved.'"

Here, we have a fundamental statement about the Christian faith, which is to believe in Jesus Christ and salvation is yours.

**Paul the Jewish Pharisee is dramatically converted to
Christianity on the road to Damascus.**

Some of the first Christian believers were horribly martyred.

Romans

§

Author and Date   The apostle Paul wrote the letter of Romans. Initially, this letter was written for the Christians living in the city of Rome. It was likely written around 58 A.D. in the city of Corinth, on one of Paul's missionary journeys.

Synopsis   The letter of Romans is one of the greatest writings in the entire Bible because it gives the reader an excellent overview of the Christian faith. Initially, it was written by the apostle Paul to lift the spirits and comfort the Christians in Rome at a difficult time. For it was at this time there was great persecution of the church in Rome. Persecution of the Christian church was not only in Rome, but also throughout the Roman Empire. Interestingly, Paul being a Roman citizen, and a Christian leader, longed to preach in Rome and encourage this church. He finally did visit Rome and proclaim the Gospel message but unfortunately many historians believe he was also martyred there. The letter of Romans tells us about many key points of the Christian faith, but its number one emphasis is about *righteousness*, the *righteousness* of the eternal God and the *righteousness* that is given to all people through Jesus Christ. The epistle of Romans is a spiritually rich and historical book, and one that should be studied by all believers.

Notable Verses
Romans 3:9-11
"What shall we conclude then? Are we any better? Not at all! We have already made the statement that Jews and Gentiles alike are all under sin. As it is written: 'There is no one righteous, not even one; there is no one who understands, no one who seeks God.'"

Here we learn that in the sight of God all are imperfect and sin, and we lack the understanding of truth. We can gain truth and understanding from God if we ask.

Romans 3:21
"But now a righteousness from God apart from the law, has been made known, to which the Law and Prophets testify."
In this verse, we understand until the time of Christ, man was under the judgment of the '*Law of Moses*' and its strict virtues, but now in Christ we can obtain true righteousness before God. This righteousness from God is freely given to us.

Romans 3:23
"For all have sinned and fall short of the glory of God."
Every man and woman is imperfect and in need of a Savior to bring them close to God. This can only be found in Christ.

Romans 5:8
"But God demonstrates his own love for us in this: while we were still sinners, Christ died for us."
God loves his creation, which is man, and even though we were far from Him, Christ brings us close to Him.

Romans 6:23
"For the wages of sin is death, but the gift of God is eternal life in Christ Jesus our Lord."
In this famous verse of scripture, we understand that sin in our lives leads to sorrow, and even death, but in Christ Jesus wholeness and blessing is ours.

Romans 8:9
"You however, are controlled not by the sinful nature, but by the Spirit, if the Spirit of God lives in you. And if anyone does not have the Spirit of Christ, he does not belong to Christ."
In this great verse, we understand that the "*Spirit of God*" is central to the life of a believer. To be a true Christian is to have Him dwell within you.

Romans 8:28

"And we know that in all things God works for the good of those who love him, who have been called according to his purpose."

When we walk with the Lord in this life, we can have complete confidence that whatever happens in our lives, ultimately good will come to us.

Romans 8:37-39

"For I am convinced that neither death nor life, neither angels nor demons, neither the present nor the future, nor any powers, neither height, nor depth, nor anything else in all creation, will be able to separate us from the love of God that is in Christ Jesus our Lord."

There is positively nothing in all of heaven and earth that can come in between God and his people, nothing!

Romans 10:9-10

"If you confess with your mouth, 'Jesus is Lord,' and believe in your heart that God raised Him from the dead, you will be saved! For it is with your heart that you believe and are justified, and it is with your mouth that you confess and are saved."

Salvation is an easy and free gift to obtain from God, but sometimes difficult to honor in our lives as a believer. The verbal confession of a person is often needed to obtain the blessings of God.

Romans 12:1-2

"Therefore, I urge you, brothers and sisters, in view of God's mercy, to offer your bodies as a living sacrifice, holy and pleasing to God, this is your true and proper worship. Do not conform to the pattern of this world, but be transformed by the renewing of your mind. Then you will be able to test and approve what God's will is, his good, pleasing and perfect will."

In this great verse of scripture we see that offering ourselves to God fully and finding his will for our lives is the most important thing we can do before Him.

The Apostle Paul wrote much of the New Testament, as 13 books are attributed to him. He preached about the 'Good News' of Jesus Christ throughout the Roman Empire, often in city courtyards and synagogues like depicted here in this picture. One of Paul's greatest writings was his letter to the Romans.

1ˢᵗ Corinthians

§

Author and Date   The apostle Paul was the author of the letter of 1ˢᵗ Corinthians. The city of Corinth was located in Greece. The letter of 1ˢᵗ Corinthians was written around 55 A.D. from the city of Ephesus.

Synopsis   The city of Corinth was a wealthy trading port in the Roman Empire during the time this letter was written. Interestingly, it was known throughout the Roman world as a sinful and wicked city. The apostle Paul started the church in Corinth and felt obligated throughout his life to be a spiritual father to these new Christians. While on a later missionary journey Paul received some troubling news about this church. He learned there was sexual immorality, abuse of spiritual gifts and a poor Christian witness to the pagan culture. Paul also discovered there was immaturity among the leaders, which caused great division in the church. With all these problems Paul needed to write to them and encourage them to live right. He addressed the Corinthians directly about these issues and encouraged them to remain faithful to the initial teachings and standards they received from him. He also embellished them to keep Christ central to their '*Faith*' and not to embrace the carnal teachings of men. 1ˢᵗ Corinthians also gives us some basic Christian doctrine on things like marriage and singlehood, food, the believer's freedom, communion, spiritual gifts and the Christian's resurrection with the eternal body.

NOTABLE VERSES
1 Corinthians 2:9
However, it is written: "No eye has seen, no ear has heard, no mind has conceived what God has prepared for those who love Him, but God has revealed it to us through His Spirit."

In this verse we see that when we have the '*Spirit of God*' living inside us. We have significant wisdom available to us and can obtain wisdom about all things, for the '*Spirit of God*' knows everything.

1 Corinthians 6:19
"Do you not know that your body is a temple of the Holy Spirit, who is in you, whom you have received from God? You are not your own; you were bought at a price. Therefore honor God with your body."

We see a powerful truth here about what a believer has, and is! The '*Spirit of God*' literally dwells in us, giving us all we need to live the life God has called us to, but it was given to us at a great price. The price was the life, death and resurrection of Christ.

The gifts of the Holy Spirit are taught in 1ˢᵗ Corinthians 12. The dove seen here in this picture is a reference to the Holy Spirit.

1 Corinthians 10:23
"Everything is permissible," but not everything is beneficial.
In this verse of scripture, we learn about the enormous freedom we believers have in Christ. But like all freedoms they must be tempered with wisdom and restraint.

1 Corinthians 13:4-7
"Love is patient, love is kind. It does not envy, it does not boast, it is not proud. It is not rude, it is not self-seeking, it is not easily angered, and it keeps no record of wrongs. Love does not delight in evil but rejoices with the truth. It always protects, always trusts, always hopes, and always perseveres."
In this famous scripture we see a significant revelation of what *Love* truly is, *Love* between God and man, and love between human beings.

1 Corinthians 15:3-4
"For what I received I passed on to you as of first importance: that Christ died for our sins according to the Scriptures, that he was buried, that he was raised on the third day according to the Scriptures."
The main reason Christ came to us 2000 thousand years ago was to die for our sins. Notice in this verse it was all according to scripture. Everything He did was backed up by Bible prophecy, and God the Father's will.

2ⁿᵈ Corinthians

§

Author and Date   The apostle Paul wrote the letter of 2ⁿᵈ Corinthians. The epistle was likely written around 55 A.D. probably from the city of Ephesus and was probably written within months of his 1ˢᵗ letter to the Corinthians.

Synopsis   The apostle Paul started the Corinthian church and lived there for over a year. In his 2ⁿᵈ letter to the Corinthians he exhorts them to remain faithful to the original Christian teachings they received from him when he was there, and especially to be aware of the false apostles and teachers who had crept into this church. In this 2ⁿᵈ letter Paul is encouraged by the Corinthians attitude towards him and his writings. Especially, when it relates to him being defamed by the false apostles who had encouraged the new believers in Corinth to disassociate themselves with him. The mighty apostle Paul in this letter also begins to clarify his worldwide ministry. As always he exhorts all people to embrace Christ and his righteousness, even over the Law of Moses. Paul teaches that when anyone embraces Christ and his righteousness, he exchanges his sin for God's holiness, and even becomes a '*new creation*,' a whole new person. Paul goes on to explain in 2ⁿᵈ Corinthians when a person becomes this new creation, generosity should be a significant earmark of their new life. Throughout this letter, one of the main themes Paul wants to get across to the Corinthians is not to accept the false teachings of others who do not practice a sound biblical faith. At the conclusion of this letter, Paul pressures the Corinthians to examine themselves fully to see if they are even true Christians, as he reminds those who are genuine believers that God's love and peace is with them.

NOTABLE VERSES

2 Corinthians 1:18
"For no matter how many promises God has made, they are yes in Christ!"
In this verse we understand that many of the promises God has given to people are ours for the taking. God has given these magnificent promises to us to be used for His glory first, and then our own benefit.

2 Corinthians 3:3
"You are a letter from Christ, the result of our ministry, written not with ink but the Spirit of the living God, not on tablets of stone but on tablets of human hearts."
Here we see the importance of being faithful to God in our spirits and minds, and not to be like many in the Old Testament who only followed God in the flesh.

2 Corinthians 5:17
"Therefore, if anyone is in Christ, he is a new creation, the old has gone, the new has come"
In this great verse we see that when one becomes a Christian he is a new creature, literally, a *'new creation,'* being able to obtain all the blessings found in Christ!

2 Corinthians 5:21
"God made him who had no sin to be sin for us, so that in Him we might become the righteousness of God."
When we exchange our imperfect life for the life of Christ, we find a righteousness that God readily accepts.

2 Corinthians 9:6
"Whoever sows sparingly will also reap sparingly, and whoever sows generously will also reap generously"
In this verse we see the principle of sowing and reaping. Whatever we give, if we give in abundance then great abundance will return to us, whether it is money, friendship, love, or any substance of life.

2 Corinthians 12:9
But he said to me, "My grace is sufficient for you, for my power is made perfect in weakness." Therefore I will boast all the more gladly about my weaknesses, so that Christ's power may rest on me. That is why, for Christ's sake, I delight in

weaknesses, in insults, in hardships, in persecutions, in difficulties. For when I am weak, then I am strong.

In this verse we learn that when we are weak in life we can lean on God to make us strong which is really not a bad place to be in life, for often we rely on our own strength to get through life when all we have to do is humble ourselves before God and receive his strength in any matter that comes our way.

Galatians

§

Author and Date   The apostle Paul was the author of the letter to the Galatians. This region is located in modern day Turkey. This letter was written somewhere between 48 and 55 A.D.

Synopsis   The region of Galatia was made up of many Jewish and Gentile converts, this letter is not to a specific city, but to this entire region in the ancient world. At this time many recent Jewish converts were teaching the new gentile believers that they had to follow the laws of Moses and other traditions of Judaism to be in right standing with God. However, in this letter Paul asserts that it is in *'Christ alone'* we are justified before God. This was a significant theological battle in the 1ˢᵗ century church and is primarily what this letter relates. Paul also vigorously defends his authority as an apostle, and the doctrines he taught, as he explains that some Jewish converts were corrupting the true gospel of Christ. He goes on to explain the dynamic truth of *'justification by faith alone'* rather than justification before God by the works of the Mosaic law, for we learn in this letter some Jewish converts of this time proclaiming the *'Law of Moses'* as a requirement for the new Christians, which went against all 'New Testament' teaching. The crux of Paul's teaching to the Galatians was the believer in Christ was free to live a holy and good life. However, Paul reminds the Galatians to stand strong in their freedom, not as an excuse to sin and gratify one's lower nature, but rather it is an opportunity to freely love God, and your fellow man. In this letter he explains that when a person is *'in Christ'* there is a war going on between our carnal nature and our spiritual life. He goes onto explain the fruits of the carnal nature are obvious, but the fruit of the believer is love, joy, peace, patience, kindness, faithfulness, gentleness and self-control. At the end of the letter, Paul reiterates that the Christian is a new creature, a *'new creation,'* and as a new creature in Christ the ways of living in the past are meaningless compared to how we should live now.

Notable Verses

Galatians 2:16

"Know that a man is not justified by observing the law, but by faith in Jesus Christ. So we, too, have put our faith in Christ Jesus that we may be justified by faith in Christ and not by observing the law, because by observing the law no one will be justified."

In this verse we learn that obtaining righteousness before God by trying to be godly is futile. For centuries the Jews tried to be righteous by obeying the laws of Moses and it rarely worked. There was a lot of judgment against the children of Israel through-out their history, but now God has made it easy for everyone to be '*holy*' before God by simply embracing Christ and the cross.

Galatians 2:20

"I have been crucified with Christ and I no longer live, but Christ lives in me. The life I live in the body, I live by faith in the Son of God, who loved me and gave himself for me."

The great truth of accepting Jesus Christ as Savior is that we live in Him, and He lives in us. In this great truth, the power of God is available to us to live good lives.

Galatians 3:11

"Clearly no one is justified before God by the law, because, 'The righteous will live by faith.'"

The celebrated reformer, Martin Luther, came to realize that the righteousness of God can be obtained by faith alone, and not by obeying laws, rules and rituals. This is how we should embrace God's righteousness.

Galatians 4:5-6

"To redeem those under law, that we might receive the full rights of sons. Because you are sons, God sent the Spirit of his Son into our hearts, the Spirit who calls out, 'Abba, Father.'"

In this great verse, we are reminded that we who are in Christ are not just lowly servants of God Almighty, but actual sons and daughters of Him, having full rights before Him as any son or daughter has in their relationship with their loving earthly father.

Galatians 5:22-23
"But the fruit of the Spirit is love, joy, peace, patience, kindness, goodness, faithfulness, gentleness and self-control. Against such things there is no law."
The by-products of living a *'Spirit-filled'* life are mentioned in this scripture. These impressive attributes should be the earmarks of any believer.

Galatians 6:7
"Do not be deceived: God cannot be mocked. A man reaps what he sows."
This is a great principle in life, if we sow good things, good things will come back to us. We have to remember that God is a *'Holy God'* and has certain standards He must adhere to, so wisdom would tell us to sow good things all throughout our lives.

Ephesians

§

Author and Date   The apostle Paul was the author of Ephesians. This letter was likely written between 60-63 A.D. while Paul was in prison in Rome. Interestingly, the city of Ephesus was a prominent trade city in the ancient world and a center for a historical pagan religion, consequently Paul spent a lot of time and resources in this great city. Ephesus today is located in modern day Turkey.

Synopsis   The letter of Ephesians is primarily about equipping and maturing the believer. In writing about this Paul reminds us of exactly how valuable we are to God, and the great blessing we have through Christ Jesus. In these great blessings we have in Christ we see the inner workings and objectives of the body of Christ. We also learn in this letter when we actively function in the body of Christ there comes Christian maturity and the ability to become true children of God. Christian standards and creeds are also emphasized throughout this epistle which makes it an indispensable book for those that want to grow in the Lord. Moreover, as we read this letter Paul often states the power the believer has in Christ, and with this power the Christian can grow mightily in faith. Towards the end of this letter Paul gives us some excellent insight to our daily lives especially in dealing with spiritual warfare, which affects all of us. In this teaching the apostle Paul uses the example of a Roman soldier in giving us an idea about the spiritual warfare that confronts a believer. Throughout this letter Paul encourages all Christians to help their fellow believers stand true and strong in God's will.

Notable Verses

Ephesians 1:3
"Blessed to the God and Father of our Lord Jesus Christ, who has blessed us in the heavenly realms with every spiritual blessing in Christ."
When we are in Christ all the blessings of heaven are ours like peace, joy and wholeness.

Ephesians 1:18-19
"I pray also that the eyes of your heart may be enlightened in order that you may know the hope to which he has called you, the riches of his glorious inheritance in the saints, and his incomparably great power for us who believe"
The greatest inheritance we can have in life is the one from God, for in it there is power for all things pertaining to life.

Ephesians 2:8-10
"For it is by grace you have been saved, through faith, and not from yourselves, for it is the gift of God, not by works, so that no one can boast! For we are God's workmanship, created in Christ Jesus to do good works, which God prepared in advance for us to do."
Salvation and heaven are a free gift from God, given to all who embrace Christ and the Cross. In our acceptance of him, God has plans for our lives, but it is our job to find out what that job is. We literally are God's very own project, and while God is working on us, we can be working toward His chief purpose for our lives.

Ephesians 3:20
"Now to Him who is able to do exceedingly, abundantly above all we ask or imagine, according to his power that is work within us, to him be the glory in the church and in Christ Jesus throughout all generations, for ever and ever."
God's power dwells within the believer in the person of the Holy Spirit to do mighty things!

Ephesians 4:4-6
"There is one body and one Spirit, just as you were called to one hope when you were called, one Lord, one faith, one baptism; one God and Father of all, who is over all and through all and in all"

The '*Body of Christ*' is immense. It covers all believers throughout the earth regardless of what denomination they belong to.

Ephesians 4:30-32
"And do not grieve the Holy Spirit of God, with whom you were sealed for the day of redemption. Get rid of all bitterness, rage and anger, brawling and slander, along with every form of malice. Be kind and compassionate to one another, forgiving each other, just as in Christ God forgave you."
The Holy Spirit can help a believer get rid of all the negative emotions that come against us in this life! *Rage and anger* are two emotions that are very destructive in our lives and need to be constantly fought against. As noted in this scripture we should always try to be kind and gracious to people just as God is always kind and loving towards us.

Ephesians 6:10
"Finally, be strong in the Lord and in his mighty power. Put on the full armor of God, so that you can take your stand against the devil's schemes. For our struggle is not against flesh and blood, but against the rulers, against the authorities, against the powers of this dark world and against the spiritual forces of evil in the heavenly realms. Therefore put on the full armor of God, so that when the day of evil comes, you may be able to stand your ground, and after you have done everything, to stand."
In this verse we are once again reminded to rely upon the Lord and his strength and power throughout our lives. We are also told about the spiritual aspects to our life here on earth, and that many of our struggles are of spiritual nature and not fleshly. In the spiritual struggles we have in life we should always put on the armor God has given to us. The two most important things we can embrace in our spiritual lives are Faith and Prayer.

Philippians

§

Author and Date   The apostle Paul was the author of the letter to the Philippians. This city is located in modern day Greece and written around 61 A.D., likely from Rome.

Synopsis   The letter to the Philippians is an uplifting writing acknowledging the church's quality growth in faith and generosity. Although persecution of the church was going on throughout the Roman Empire, the new church in Philippi was strong and staying faithful to Christ and sound doctrine. The letter tells about the believer's life in Christ and the profound insight of it. Paul explains to the reader there is great joy and peace for the believer wherever they are, because Jesus Christ dwells within them through the Holy Spirit. The knowledge of Christ living in us is a great revelation. In this revelation we should externally live good lives, including embracing *'humility'* as Christ did, who being God, humbled himself for our sakes. In our humility, we can be powerful servants to both man and God.

NOTABLE VERSES
Philippians 4:4
"Rejoice in the Lord always. I will say it again: Rejoice!"
Here is something believers should always do, and that is to *'Rejoice'* in all things!

Philippians 4:6-7
"Do not be anxious about anything, but in everything, by prayer and supplication, with thanksgiving, present your requests to God. And the peace of God, which transcends all understanding, will guard your hearts and your minds in Christ Jesus."

In this verse we learn about a great truth in scripture, which is to never worry or be anxious about our lives. If we walk with God in this life, we need only to trust in Him, and all will be well. We can also lean on his glorious presence in our hearts at all times. This will give us the peace and strength that is needed regardless of what happens throughout our day.

Philippians 4:13
"I can do all things through Christ who gives me strength."
This is an exciting promise for us, for God does give us strength to meet any problem we face in life, all we have to do is ask Him. The word *"Him"* here is a mention of *"Christ"* and the powerful anointing. Often in life we try to do things on our own, and we sometimes fail, but as this verse states; *If we do things through Him we will have the victory!*

Colossians

§

Author and Date   The apostle Paul was the author of the letter of Colossians. The city of Colossae is located in modern day Turkey. Paul may have had some help from his assistant Timothy in writing this letter. Colossians was likely written between A.D. 58-62 from Rome.

Synopsis   The book of Colossians is primarily about the supremacy of Christ in our lives and the principles of Christian living. Paul reminds us that Jesus Christ should be pre-eminent in our lives and not the vain philosophies of the world. In the letter of Colossians, Paul emphasizes that all believers are equal in Jesus Christ. At the time of the writing of Colossians there was a clear deviation from orthodox teaching by some in this community of believers, so in the letter of Colossians, Paul encourages them to be faithful to sound doctrines of the Christian faith. There was a heresy being taught in this local church called '*Gnosticism*' and also a teaching by some Jews that believers in Christ had to be circumcised and follow the '*Law of Moses*' to have right standing with God. Paul fights these heresies and as always reiterates that '*faith*' in Christ is all that is needed to have right standing with God. In this letter, Paul also emphasizes a basic doctrine of the Christian faith, which is '*Christ is Deity*' in bodily form.

Notable Verses
Colossians 1:15-16
"He is the image of the invisible God, the firstborn over all creation. For by Him all things were created: things in heaven and on earth, visible and invisible, whether thrones or powers or rulers or authorities; all things were created by Him and for Him."

Here, we learn in this scripture the true personhood of Christ. He was the eternal God come to mankind.

Colossians 2:9
"For in Christ all the fullness of God lives in bodily form"
We understand that Jesus Christ was God clothed in flesh. In Him, we understand that the Creator got as close to humanity as He could, while still remaining Deity!

Colossians 3:12-13
"Therefore, as God's chosen people, holy and dearly loved, clothe you with compassion, kindness, humility, gentleness and patience. Bear with each other and forgive whatever grievances you may have against one another. Forgive as the Lord forgave you."
The believer should be a compassionate, kind and patient person, for if we partake in these magnificent virtues, compassion and kindness will be shown to us by both God and man.

1ˢᵗ Thessalonians

§

Author and Date   The letter of 1st Thessalonians was written by the apostle Paul. Thessaloniki is located in modern Greece today. Paul was the original founder of this church and wrote this letter to them around 50 A.D.

Synopsis   The return of Jesus Christ to earth and living a Godly life were the main concerns of the church of Thessalonica. In this letter the great apostle Paul tried to give clear definitions of these subjects. The first three chapters are about Paul longing to visit the church in Thessalonica but not being able to because Satan himself stops him. Paul cared deeply for the Thessalonians and was encouraged to hear how well they had been doing, which was good news to the apostle because many of the other churches were experiencing great problems. Toward the end of the letter Paul instructs the believers in Thessalonica on how to live Godly lives in Christ Jesus, and then goes on to instruct them about some misconceptions they had about the end times. He explains to them that believers who have died in Christ will come with the Lord when He returns to earth, and regardless of where a believer is, he or she will always be with the Lord. At the conclusion of the letter new Christians are encouraged to live holy and good lives.

Notable Verses
1 Thessalonians 4:14-17
"We believe that Jesus died and rose again and so we believe that God will bring with Jesus those who have fallen asleep in him. According to the Lord's own word, we tell you that we who are still alive, who are left till the coming of the Lord, will certainly not precede those who have fallen asleep. For the Lord himself will come down from heaven, with a loud command, with the voice of the archangel and with

the trumpet call of God, and the dead in Christ will rise first. After that, we who are still alive and are left will be caught up together with them in the clouds to meet the Lord in the air. And so we will be with the Lord forever."

In this verse we see what happens to those who have died in Christ. We also have insight into the earthly return of Jesus Christ. Even though Christians have differing interpretations of this scripture, and the others concerning the end of the age, we can all agree the most prominent part of this passage is the last statement which says "We will be with the Lord forever," in this we find extraordinary comfort.

1 Thessalonians 5:1
"Now brothers, about times and seasons we do not need to write you, for you know very well that the day of the Lord will come like a thief in the night"

In the day and times we are living we often hear about the end of the world and the return of the Lord. We should always be cautious in listening to people about these things for no one knows the exact day or hour when Christ returns to earth to set up his earthly kingdom. In this revelation, we should live such good lives that regardless of when He comes all will be well with us.

The apostle Paul wrote some of his letters to the Church while in Roman prisons.

2ⁿᵈ Thessalonians

§

Author and Date   The letter of 2nd Thessalonians was written by the apostle Paul. It was likely written around 51-52 A.D. probably in the city of Corinth.

Synopsis   The Christians in the Thessalonian church thought the "*End of the World*" was at hand. Some even thought the "*Day of The Lord*" had already occurred. In this letter, Paul wrote to this church and gave them sound doctrine about this issue. Also, this church was facing persecution and many needed wisdom and encouragement at this difficult time. Paul, as usual, encourages the Thessalonian believers to be strong in the basic doctrines of the Faith.

NOTABLE VERSES

2 Thessalonians 1:6-7
"God is just: He will pay back trouble to those who trouble you and give relief to you who are troubled, and to us as well. This will happen when the Lord Jesus is revealed from heaven in blazing fire with powerful angels."
In this verse we see Paul reminding believers that God sees our struggles and persecutions in this life and that He will intervene. We also get a glimpse of how the Lord will return from heaven to earth and the power and glory will be seen.

2 Thessalonians 2:13
"But we ought to always thank God for you, brothers loved by the Lord, because from the beginning God chose you to be saved through the sanctifying work of the Spirit and through belief in the truth."

In this verse we see how God ordained people to be saved, and once saved; the *'Holy Spirit'* does his great work in the believer. This is done by the *'Spirit of God'* dwelling in the believer to give him strength and power to live a Godly life.

2 Thessalonians 3:3
"But the Lord is faithful, and he will strengthen and protect you from the evil one."
The believer who walks with the Lord in this life can always count on God to strengthen and encourage him, and even protect him from evil.

Titus

§

Author and Date   The apostle Paul was the author of this letter, which was written around 66 A.D. The name Titus is a Roman word that may mean *"Title of honor."* Titus was an early leader in the church. Paul wrote to this church leader when he was on one of his missionary journeys.

Synopsis   The letter to Titus is known as one of the *'Pastoral Epistles'* because it primarily concerns us with church leadership and sound doctrinal issues. The epistle was written by Paul to encourage his Christian brother Titus, who was a gentile believer. We learn in this letter Paul had left him in Crete to lead the church which Paul had established on one of his missionary journeys. This letter instructs Titus about what qualifications are required for leaders in the local Church, which was needed at this time in the history of the Church. Paul also writes he wants Titus to return to him for a visit so that he can personally encourage him in the *'Faith.'* The reason for this was that Paul felt it was his personal responsibility to help develop Titus to be a great Christian leader. Interestingly, Paul more than likely led Titus to Christianity under his preaching, and wanted to make sure the young believer was growing strong in the things of God.

NOTABLE VERSES
Titus 1:5
"The reason I left you in Crete was that you might straighten out what was left unfinished and appoint elders in every town, as I directed you."
In the first century each town only had local elders to minister to the people. They usually met in someone's house to pray, read scripture and conduct church business.

Titus 2:10
"So that in every way they will make the teaching about God our Savior attractive."
God wants his people to make the *'Christian Faith'* as attractive and appealing as possible to everyone, while still remaining true to sound doctrine.

Titus 3:1
"Remind the people to be subject to rulers and authorities, to be obedient, to be ready to do whatever is good, to slander no one, to be peaceable and considerate, and to show true humility toward all men."
God wants his people to be good citizens wherever they may live in the world. Along with being good people, He wants us to live in peace and humility before everyone. To be considerate and humble is not a sign of weakness but of extraordinary strength when exercised properly.

Philemon

§

Author and Date   The author of the letter of Philemon was the apostle Paul. The name Philemon means *"Affectionate."* This letter was written around 60 A.D. when he was in prison.

Synopsis   The letter to Philemon is a short letter primarily dealing with the subject of slavery, something that was particularly common in the first century. The slave owner in this letter was a wealthy man named Philemon, who was also a leader in the Church. He had a slave named Onesimus, who stole from him and then ran away, which was a serious crime in the Roman Empire. Onesimus went to Rome to seek Paul's help, so Paul wrote this letter to his friend and Christian brother Philemon on behalf of Onesimus, the slave. Paul encourages Philemon to treat his slave Onesimus first as a brother in Christ, and then secondly as a slave. Paul warns all slave owners that they have to be good to their slaves, especially to those who fear God and are in the Christian Faith. Interestingly, to the modern reader of this text, Paul never condemns the institution of slavery, but encourages both slave owner and slave to remember they are fellow heirs of salvation in Christ. Although this contains writings about slave master and slave it can also be a witness to us also about the relationship between a Christian boss and his employees, and the fair treatment both sides should receive in the daily dealings of this relationship.

Notable Verses
Philemon 6
"I pray that your partnership with us in the faith may be effective in deepening your understanding of every good thing we have in Christ." Your love has given

me great joy and encouragement, because you, brother, have refreshed the hearts of the saints.

In this verse, we are exhorted to always be on the lookout for an opportunity to share the exciting *'Faith'* that we have. This is God's will for all believers, to be able to give a good accounting of the ardent hope we have in Christ Jesus.

Philemon 7
"Your love has given me great joy and encouragement, because you, brother, have refreshed the hearts of the Lord's people."

In this scripture we learn that it is important to always strengthen and encourage our fellow believers, knowing full well that the trials and tribulations we are going through they are also going through.

Philemon 19
"I, Paul, am writing with my own hand"

The apostle Paul wrote most of his letters himself, which is refreshing to know. He wrote not only with his own knowledge of the subjects, but more importantly, under the direction of the Spirit of God.

Hebrews

§

Author and Date   We do not know who wrote Hebrews. It may have been the apostle Paul, or Apollos or Barnabas, but the writer must have been a Jew, because of the title and emphasis of the letter. The writing was probably written around 65 A.D.

Synopsis   The letter of Hebrews was directed toward Jewish Christians, because many were drifting back into the traditions and ancient rituals of Judaism. Throughout this epistle the writer always emphasizes the importance of Christ over pre-cross Judaism. Also in this letter, the author makes clear that Jesus Christ can be found throughout the writings of the Old Testament, culminating in Him being the long awaited Messiah. The writer tells us that many of the rituals and observances of Judaism symbolically point to Jesus being the Messiah, but not a Messiah like many Jews envisioned, like the military hero King David, but a Messiah who was '*God incarnate*' who brings the Kingdom of God to both Jews and Gentiles, and all of mankind. The letter of Hebrews explains to the reader using many verses of the Old Testament that Christ Jesus is far superior to anything ancient Judaism has to offer, first for the Jew and then for the Gentile. The book of Hebrews also explains to us that it was always in the heart of God that the religion or '*Faith of Abraham*' was to be for the whole world, and in Jesus Christ the dream of God is fulfilled.

NOTABLE VERSES
Hebrews 1:1-2
"In the past God spoke to our forefathers through the prophets at many times and in various ways, but in these last days he has spoken to us by his Son, whom he appointed heir of all things, and through whom he made the universe."

In the time before Christ, God used the '*Jewish Faith*' to present himself to the World, but now in Christ, everyone can have the full and complete knowledge of God.

Hebrews 4:14-16
"Therefore, since we have a great high priest who has gone through the heavens, Jesus the Son of God, let us hold firmly to the faith we profess. For we do not have a high priest who is unable to sympathize with our weaknesses, but we have one who has been tempted in every way, just as we are—yet was without sin. Let us then approach the throne of grace with confidence, so that we may receive mercy and find grace to help us in our time of need."
One of the offices that Christ holds for us is High Priest, and unlike the High Priest of ancient times, or even today, we have full access to God 24 hours a day to help us with our needs and struggles in life.

Hebrews 11:1
"Now faith is the substance of things hoped for, and the certainty of what we do not see."
Faith is a spiritual gift and an actual substance available to us, however, like all gifts it must be exercised and used for it to be taken advantage of.

Hebrews 12:1-2
"Therefore, since we are surrounded by such a great cloud of witnesses, let us throw off everything that hinders and the sin that so easily entangles, and let us run with perseverance the race marked out for us. Let us fix our eyes on Jesus, the author and perfecter of our faith, who for the joy set before him endured the cross, scorning its shame, and sat down at the right hand of the throne of God."
We are not alone in this life. Many have gone through the same struggles and disappointments we have, most notably the *Son of God*. He empathizes with us in our ways and is always there to offer encouragement and comfort.

**In the epistle of Hebrews, the importance of Christ going to
the cross is emphasized over the Old Testament law.**

James

§

Author and Date   The author of this letter is James, who is believed to be the half-brother of Jesus Christ. In the early days of the Christian faith, this same James was the head of the Jerusalem church. The name James may mean *"may God protect."* It is believed this letter may be one the oldest letters of the New Testament and was written in Jerusalem as early as 45 A.D.

Synopsis   The letter of James is primarily written for Jewish Christians living throughout the Roman Empire. In this letter the author tells us *'works,'* or *'personal piety'* is a must for a Christian, before God and man. James emphasizes that godly actions will be an earmark of true believers, consequently one of the focal points of this epistle is that those who do not produce godly fruit in their lives may not be in the *'Faith'* at all. Because of this emphasis on *'works,'* many Christian leaders through the centuries have questioned James teachings on this subject. In the beginning of James he seems to want to impress upon everyone that authentic Christian faith must coincide directly with authentic actions. In writing about this James adds that the world is filled with wisdom, but wisdom from God is what the believer should always embrace, and in doing so the believer draws close to the Lord. In this letter there is also a rebuke for those who trust in their wealth and exploit the poor, in this, he exhorts true followers of Christ to be noble and pure, especially if they are blessed with influence and wealth. At this time in history there was great persecution against the new Christian faith, so James encourages all to be faithful in their sufferings and to always encourage one another.

Notable Verses
James 2:17-18
"In the same way, faith by itself, if it is not accompanied by action, is dead. But someone will say, 'You have faith; I have deeds.' Show me your faith without deeds, and I will show you my faith by what I do."
In this verse we see the theology of James, which emphasizes deeds or works. There is wisdom in this doctrine, for certainly acts of righteousness and charity should be a lifestyle for all believers.

James 3:5
"Likewise the tongue is a small part of the body, but it makes great boasts. Consider that a great forest is set on fire by a small spark."
There is great wisdom for everyone in this verse, the old expression *"hold your tongue"* is something we all should practice until we are sure of what we will say.

James 5:16
"The prayer of a righteous man is powerful and effective."
When we walk with the Lord, He is always readily available to answer prayer.

1ˢᵗ Peter

§

Author and Date   The author of the epistle of 1st Peter was the apostle Peter. The name Peter means *"stone"* or *"rock."* The letter of 1st Peter was likely written between 60 and 65 A.D. in the city of Rome.

Synopsis   The apostle Peter wrote this letter to Christians throughout the Roman Empire. At this time in history the church was under tremendous persecution and needed encouragement, especially from a great church leader like Peter. Peter had suffered much for being an apostle of Christ and certainly could teach and encourage the believers to remain faithful to the Lord at this time. Peter tells the persecuted believers in this letter that they should always be joyful in their lives no matter the circumstance, and if they suffer it was a privilege to suffer for Christ. Peter also emphasizes in this epistle that believers must stay strong in the face of evil and always have the eternal hope for the return of Jesus Christ.

NOTABLE VERSES
1 Peter 1:3
"Praise to the God and Father of our Lord Jesus Christ! In his great mercy he has given us new birth into a living hope through the resurrection of Jesus Christ from the dead."
In this verse we learn from Peter the *'born-again experience'* in Christ, which is for everyone!

1 Peter 1:7
"These have come that your faith, which is more precious than Gold, which perishes even though refined by fire, may prove genuine and may result in praise, glory and honor when Jesus Christ is revealed."
We learn the importance of faith in our lives, which is certainly the most important thing for believers to grow. For faith is a gift from God, and like all gifts it must be opened and used for it to be of any value.

1 Peter 1:24
"All men are like grass, and all their glory is like the flowers of the field, for the grass withers and the flowers fade away, but the Word of the Lord stands forever"!
Everything in this life is temporal, our bodies, our wealth, our homes, bank accounts, our relationships and so on, but what lasts forever is the Lord and his ways. Wisdom would tell us to put eternal things first in our lives and let all the other things come secondary.

1 Peter 2:9
"But you are a chosen people, a royal priesthood, a holy nation, a people belonging to God, that you may declare the praises of him who called you out of darkness into his wonderful light."
Here, God gives His people a dynamic indication of who they are in Christ Jesus!

1 Peter 2:24
"He himself bore our sins in his body on the tree, so that we might die to sins and live for righteousness; by his wounds you have been healed."
In this verse, we understand the crucifixion of Jesus Christ was not only for our sins to be forgiven, but also for our healing.

1 Peter 5:5
"God opposes the proud but gives grace to the humble"
We understand in this verse that humility is an outstanding virtue. Humility first before God, and then our fellow man. If we do this with sincerity and wisdom, God Himself will give us his grace and peace.

1 Peter 5:8-9

"Be self-controlled and alert. Your enemy the devil prowls around like a roaring lion looking for someone to devour. Resist him, standing firm in the faith, because you know that your brothers throughout the world are undergoing the same kind of sufferings."

The scripture here tells us that we are not alone in our struggles in our Christian life, but that other believers are going through the same things we are, and in being strong in faith, we have victory.

1Peter 5:10

"And the God of all grace, who called you to His eternal glorying Christ, after you have suffered awhile will himself restore you and make you strong, firm and steadfast"

In this verse, we can take considerable encouragement that after we stand strong through the trials that come to us in our lives, God will make us even stronger and better.

In this picture we see Peter preaching to 1st century believers, since there was no New Testament book yet or local church buildings, the leaders of the Church sent letters and writings to one another and simply read them to all the people during their worship services.

2nd Peter

§

Author and Date   The apostle Peter was the author of this letter. It was written toward the end of Peter's life. Historians believe that Peter was martyred in Rome during the reign of the Roman Emperor Nero, so it was likely he wrote 2nd Peter between 65 and 68 A.D.

Synopsis   Peter was alarmed that false teachers were beginning to infiltrate the churches. He called on Christians to grow and become strong in their faith so that they could detect and combat spreading apostasy. In this epistle, he strongly stressed two things, the authenticity of the *'Word of God'* and the sure return of the Lord. Peter knew that his time was short, and the Christians faced immediate danger, so he challenged the believers to become more mature in their faith by adding to it specific Christian virtues like *'patience'* and *'love'* so that they could become effective and productive in their knowledge of Jesus Christ. Peter also desired they become strong in their faith to withstand the false teachers that had crept in and adversely affected the churches. In his denunciation of these teachers, he describes their conduct, their characteristics, and also their ridicule of the Lord's Second Coming, consequently Peter taught that the *'Second Coming'* is the main incentive for holy living. At the end of his letter, Peter again encourages believers to grow in the grace and knowledge of our Lord and Savior Jesus Christ.

NOTABLE VERSES
2 Peter 1:3-4
"His divine power has given us everything we need for life and godliness through our knowledge of Him who called us by His own glory and goodness. Through these He has given us His very great and precious promises, so that through them you

may participate in the divine nature and escape the corruption in the world caused by evil desires."

God has given us all the tools we need to live good lives, we can only do this by the power of the Holy Spirit. We can also do this by embracing the magnificent promises found in scripture, for it is in the *'Word of God'* we can find exceptional strength and answers to help make decisions in our life. The Divine nature of God is eternal and lasts forever, but the desires we have in this life will pass away.

2 Peter 3:9

"The Lord is not slow in keeping His promise, as some understand slowness. He is patient with you, not wanting anyone to perish, but everyone to come to repentance."

In this verse, we understand the great virtue of *'patience,'* for how many times in our lives have we become impatient, worry, and make the wrong decision, so it is *'patience'* that we need in abundance. The Lord is often patient with us because he knows how imperfect we really are.

In this picture, we see Peter denying Jesus Christ on the night he was betrayed. All throughout Peter's life he was reminded of this failure, this is why he often preached and wrote about God's great mercy to all

1ˢᵗ John

§

Author and Date   The author of 1st John was the apostle John. The name John means "*the Lord is gracious.*" Interestingly, he was a first cousin of Jesus Christ so he probably knew Christ better than the other disciples. The epistle of John 1 was likely written between 85-95 A.D. from the city of Ephesus.

Synopsis   The book of 1st John confronts the religious philosophy of '*Gnosticism.*' The main philosophy of the Gnostics was '*matter*' is evil, and '*spirit*' is good, however, the actual word "*Gnosticism*" means '*knowledge.*' There were many false preachers in the early church, and this became an enormous problem, especially for the gentile believers who were not founded in Old Testament scriptures. John, being an eyewitness to the life and teachings of Christ, tried to give a straight and narrow approach to the new believers, especially in the teaching about the true person of Jesus Christ. John also emphasized that '*Love*' with godly action was the true test for someone in the Christian faith and reminded believers that if they were not practicing these attributes they may want to question their relationship with God. He also tells us that holy lives were something always to strive for, but it was often unattainable for us. In conclusion, he reminds us if we commit sins we should confess them to God and forgiveness was ours.

NOTABLE VERSES
1 John 1:9
"If we confess our sins, he is faithful and just and will forgive us our sins and purify us from all unrighteousness."
In this scripture we see the magnificent teaching in 1ˢᵗ John. Which is if we confess any sin or wrongdoing, God will forgive and restore us.

1 John 2:26

" As for you, the anointing you received from Him remains in you, and you do not need anyone to teach you, but as his anointing teaches you about all things and that anointing is real, not counterfeit, just as it has taught you to remain in him."

In this verse, we believers understand that we should always look to God first in what we learn about the Christian faith, and regardless of what any man or church denomination says, God's '*Word*' comes first.

1 John 3:1

"How great is the love the Father has lavished on us! That we should be called children of God"

What a marvelous revelation to all those in Christ. This is one of those overpowering statements that encourages everyone to feel good about self and others. We imperfect believers are not just servants of God, but his sons and daughters, being able to partake in everything that our Heavenly Father has for us.

1 John 4:4

"You, dear children, are from God and have overcome them, because the one who is in you is greater than the one who is in the world."

We see that God literally dwells in the believer. He always is able to help us in our lives so anything that happens to us can be overcome by this inner strength.

1 John 5:13

"I write these things to you who believe in the name of the Son of God so that you may know that you have eternal life. This is the confidence we have in approaching God: that if we ask anything according to his will, he hears us, and if we know that He hears us, whatever we ask, we know we have what we asked of Him"

This is always the message of John the Apostle, that if we embrace Jesus Christ, salvation is ours forever. We learn not only is eternal life ours, but we can ask God for things we need, and He will give them to us, just like a good and loving earthly father gives to his children.

1 John 5:19

"We know that we are children of God, and that the whole world is under the control of the evil one. We know also that the Son of God has come and has given us

understanding, so that we may know him who is true. And we are in him who is true by being in his Son Jesus Christ. He is the true God and eternal life."

In this verse we once again learn that we are the children of God. We develop this relationship through God the Father and come to understand this fully through Jesus Christ. One of the main truth's we learn in this relationship is that eternal life is ours forever!

1John5:20

"We know also that the Son of God has come and has given us understanding, so that we may know him who is true. And we are in him, who is true, by being in his Son Jesus Christ. He is the true God and eternal life."

Here we see an affirmation by the apostle John that if we are in Jesus Christ we have the truth of the eternal God. In this idea we learn the greatest truth of all, which is that we have eternal life in Him.

2ⁿᵈ John

Author and Date   The author of the letter of 2ⁿᵈ John was the apostle John and was most likely written about the same time as John's other letters, somewhere in between 85-95 A.D. probably from the city of Ephesus.

Synopsis   In the book of 2ⁿᵈ John he exhorts the believer not only to love God but also our fellow man. John also reiterates his stern warning to be on guard against those who preach that Jesus Christ was not raised from the dead in bodily form. The most antagonistic groups to the apostle John and the early church were the '*Gnostics*' who John frequently criticized in all his letters. The letter of 2ⁿᵈ John is not only about preaching against the Gnostics, but also other religious deceivers who were not teaching the true doctrine of Christ. These groups maintained that Jesus did not actually resurrect in the flesh, but only spiritually, which is a foundational Christian doctrine. John is also very anxious to tell true believers that they should always be aware of these false teachers and have nothing to do with them.

NOTABLE VERSES
2 John 6
"And this is love: that we walk in obedience to his commands. As you have heard from the beginning, his command is that you walk in love."
In this teaching we see that to walk in love before God, and our fellow man, is the summation of how Christians should live on the earth. To walk in love is difficult in the times we are living but it is something we should certainly strive for. If we walk in this love, then we will receive God's blessing in this life and certainly greater blessing in the next one.

2 John 7
"I say this because many deceivers, who do not acknowledge Jesus Christ as coming in the flesh, have gone out in the world; any such person is a deceiver and an anti-Christ."

We understand here that John is warning us against a significant heresy that came against the Christian church in the 1st century, and even comes today. The crux of this heresy was that Jesus was not the *'Messiah'*, that he was not the *'Christ'*, but only a prophet or good man. We who are in the Christian faith must always stand tall and remain true to the truth that he was *"Immanuel,"* God with us!

2 John 9
"Anyone who runs ahead and does not continue in the teaching of Christ does not have God; whoever continues in the teaching has both the Father and the Son."

In this powerful verse we can understand of the importance of the relationship between the Father, the Son and the believer.

3ʳᵈ John

Author and Date   The apostle John is the author of 3ʳᵈ John. This letter was most likely written at about the same time as John's other letters, between A.D. 85-95.

Synopsis   John's purpose in writing this third epistle was threefold. First, he writes to commend and encourage his co-worker, a person named Gaius, for being hospitable to itinerant Christian leaders who were traveling to preach the Gospel. Secondly, he condemns the behavior of an egotistical leader who had taken over one of the churches, and whose behavior was directly opposed to everything that the apostle and what the *"Word"* stood for. Thirdly, he commends the example of a man named Demetrius who had a good reputation from everyone. As John is writing directly to Gaius, who was a leader with some wealth and distinction in the city, he specifically commends Gaius's care and hospitality to the Christian messengers, whose mission was to take the Gospel from place to place. John exhorts Gaius to continue to do these generous acts and not to imitate a man called Diotrephes, who had taken over the leadership of a church in Asia. This man not only refused to recognize John's authority as an apostle, but also did not receive his letters and submission to his instructions.

Notable Verses
3 John 2
"Beloved, I wish above all things that you may prosper and be in health, even as your soul prospers."
In this great verse we learn God wants us to be spiritually successful, and also physically healthy and prosperous in all our ways. When we understand that God created

us as a triune being having a body, soul and spirit we can know that He is always concerned with all aspects of our life!

3 John 11
"Dear friend, do not imitate what is evil but what is good. Anyone who does what is good is from God. Anyone who does what is evil has not seen God."

As believers we must always try to embrace good over evil in our lives. This not only pleases God but gives Him a good name before our fellow man. Often times in the world in which we live it is hard to do the right thing, but it is beneficial to always do it, not only when someone is watching you, but also when no one is watching. If we make doing good a lifestyle practice it will get easier for us in all situations.

Jude

§

Author and Date   The author of the epistle of Jude was likely Jude, the brother of James, and the half-brother of Jesus. The name Jude can mean *"to praise."* This letter was written sometime around 65 A.D.

Synopsis   The epistle of Jude is one of the smallest books in the entire Bible, but an important one for us because it involves remaining true to God's righteousness. The epistle of Jude also gives us some insight into a few intriguing Old Testament stories. The Christian church actually started at the day of Pentecost. So in this epistle, Jude tells us to be aware of false teaching and false prophets who have gained entrance into the church. In Jude's writings about heresy and the judgment to follow, he reminds us from some of the stories in the Old Testament; like Sodom and Gomorrah, the ways of Cain, and the Israelites who rebelled against God. In Jude, we are also exhorted to be *'Defenders of the Faith'* at all times, the *Faith* that exemplifies sound Christian doctrine which was taught by Jesus Christ himself, and later by the apostles.

NOTABLE VERSES
Jude 17-19
"But, dear friends, remember what the apostles of our Lord Jesus Christ foretold. They said to you; 'In the last times there will be scoffers who will follow their own ungodly desires.' These are the men who divide you, who follow mere natural instincts and do not have the Spirit."
In this verse we have a good reminder of the times we are living in today. People, both in the church and outside the church have turned away from good and decent teachings on how we should live our lives. Everyone wants to live a long, healthy and prosperous life. This can be obtained if we follow the ways the Lord has given us.

Jude 24-25

"To him who is able to keep you from falling and to present you before his glorious presence without fault and with great joy. To the only God our Savior be glory, majesty, power and authority, through Jesus Christ our Lord, before all ages, now and forevermore! Amen."

Here, we have a glimpse of the judgment seat of Christ. Although we do not fully understand how God's judgment day will be formatted, we do have some ideas revealed to us in scriptures like this one. One basic teaching is that every knee will bow, and every tongue confess that Jesus Christ is Lord. We will do this in either honor or love for Him, or in fear and trembling. The choice is ours.

Revelation

§

Author and Date   The author of the book of Revelation was the apostle John. The word Revelation means to *"disclose or reveal something."* This book was likely written around 90 A.D. on the island of Patmos, some 40 miles from the ancient city of Ephesus.

Synopsis   The book of Revelation is a greatly discussed and misunderstood book. In the late 1ˢᵗ century there was great persecution against the Church and many Christians at this time believed the end of the world was eminent, with the final battle between God and Satan at hand. Consequently, this book is written with dramatic words, prophecy, and symbolism, giving us a vivid story of John's revelation to believers. The book of Revelation is filled with secretive images and dramatic pictures of things to come, but throughout this writing it always reminds the reader of the coming judgment upon those who reject God and his Word.   The book of Revelation gives us colorful descriptions of the visions the apostle John received while he was on the island of Patmos. It speaks of the end times, the final years before Christ's return to earth when God establishes a new heaven and earth. The book begins with seven letters being sent to seven different churches in Asia Minor, and then moves on to some of the more famous descriptions of this writing like; *"the mark of the beast,"* the number *"666"* being placed on nonbelievers, the great tribulation, the war of Armageddon, angelic beings bringing dramatic judgments to the earth, Satan and his angels being thrown into hell, the *'Great White Throne Judgment*, and the city of God coming to earth. In reading Revelation we must remember this book can offer the reader many differing theories and interpretations of things to come, but the underlying emphasis of the book is the *'revelation'* to everyone about the sovereignty of the Lord God over all things!

NOTABLE VERSES
Revelation 4:8
"Holy, Holy, Holy is the Lord God Almighty, who was, who is, and is to come"
In this powerful verse we see the nature of the true and living God! He is Holy! He is everlasting with no beginning and no end! He is the great I Am!

Revelation 5:5
"Do not weep! See the Lion of the tribe of Judah, the root of David, has triumphed. He is able to open the scroll and its seven seals."
Here, we see Jesus Christ as the triumphant King of heaven and earth. He was descended from King David, and the Hebrew tribe of Judah which fulfilled the ancient prophecies about where the *'Messiah'* would come from.

Revelation 13:16-17
"He also forced everyone, small and great, rich and poor, free and slave, to receive a mark on his right hand or on his forehead, so that no one could buy or sell unless he had the mark, which is the name of the beast or the number of his name."
When the Anti-Christ reigns on earth he will demand full subservience from all peoples.

Revelation19:16
On his robe and on his thigh he has this name: "King of Kings and Lord of Lords."
In this scripture we learn a revered name attributed to the Jesus Christ. This is a title that will be given him fully during His 1000 year reign in the millennium kingdom.

Revelation 20:11
"Then I saw a great white throne and him who was seated on it. Earth and sky fled from his presence, and there was no place for them."
In this verse we get a glimpse of the judgment seat of God Almighty. All of creation will bow in obedience to Him on that day.

Revelation 21:1
"Then I saw a new heaven and a new earth, for the first heaven and the first earth had passed away, and there was no longer any sea."
We learn in this verse that God, in the future, will give us a new heaven and earth that will be infinitely better than the one we have now.

Revelation 22:12

"Behold I am coming soon! My reward is with me, and I will give to everyone according to what he was done. I am the Alpha and Omega, the First and the last, the beginning and the End."

We learn in this verse that Jesus Christ will literally return to earth and bring with him eternal rewards for the faithful.

**Jesus Christ will return to earth one day and reward
the faithful and set up his earthly kingdom!**

In this Bible commentary, it was the author's hope that all may find peace and love in the One who was *'The Word who became Flesh and dwelled among us.'* The *Nicene Creed* is a great foundational statement about the Christian faith, in a nutshell, and often recited in many churches every Sunday. The initial *Nicene Creed* was written in 325 A.D., but below is a later version of the Creed which will inspire all who read it.

Nicene Creed

We believe in one God the Father almighty, maker of heaven and earth and of all things visible and invisible. And in one Lord Jesus Christ, the Son of God, the only-begotten, begotten of the Father before all ages; Light of Light, true God of true God, begotten, not made, of one essence with the Father, by whom all things were made. Who for us men and for our salvation came down from heaven, and was incarnate by the Holy Spirit and the Virgin Mary, and became man. He was crucified for us under Pontius Pilate, and suffered and was buried, and on the third day He rose again according to the Scriptures, He ascended into heaven and now sits at the right hand of the Father. We believe He shall come again with glory to judge the living and the dead and of His kingdom there shall be no end! We believe in the Holy Spirit, the Lord, the Giver of life, who proceeded from the Father, who with the Father and the Son together is worshipped and glorified, who was spoken by the prophets. We believe in one holy universal and apostolic church, in one baptism for the forgiveness of sins, in the resurrection of the dead and eternal life in the age to come. Amen

Made in the USA
San Bernardino, CA
01 June 2020

72339318R00115